Patty,
   Here is another book
for you to enjoy. Hope it
lifts your spirits.
          Love. Nancy

The HEART
OF A
FATHER

The HEART OF A FATHER

true stories of inspiration and encouragement

Compiled By
WAYNE HOLMES

BETHANY HOUSE PUBLISHERS

Minneapolis, Minnesota

Published by Bethany House Publishers
A Ministry of Bethany Fellowship International
11400 Hampshire Avenue South
Bloomington, Minnesota 55438
www.bethanyhouse.com

Printed in the United States of America by
Bethany Press International, Bloomington, Minnesota 55438

Library of Congress Cataloging-in-Publication Data

The heart of a father : true stories of inspiration and encouragement ; compiled by Wayne Holmes.
    p. cm.
    ISBN 0-7642-2543-X (pbk.)
    1. Fathers—Religious life. I. Holmes, Wayne.
    BV4529.17 .H43   2002
    242'.6421—dc21   2002001340

TO
my dad,
Denver Holmes, Jr.,
for living a life of faith;
and
to my four children
for giving me the opportunity
to experience the joys of fatherhood

ACKNOWLEDGMENTS

I also want to acknowledge the following people who gave their love and support for this project.

Special thanks to my wife, Linda, for believing in me and for encouraging me through difficult times.

To my mother, Joyce Holmes, for her loving support in all my endeavors.

Thanks to Bob Hostetler for being a mentor and friend. Your guidance proved invaluable in launching my writing career and also this book.

Special thanks and hugs to my friend, teacher, and loyal supporter, Cec Murphey; you've been a godsend.

To Michael Brewer I extend warm thanks for being a buddy and advocate. Thanks for all the lunch meetings and helpful insights you passed my way.

I owe a debt of gratitude to the Greater Cincinnati Christian Writers' Fellowship for the valuable insights they've shared.

To my cousin, Tim Bullock, I extend my warmest appreciation for believing in me and for standing beside me.

To other family members and friends, I want to say thanks for your presence in my life.

I am especially grateful to Steve Laube and Bethany House Publishers for allowing this project to take wings.

Finally, to all the writers whose words appear in this book, thank you for sharing your stories.

CONTENTS

SECTION FOUR:

THE TEACHING OF A FATHER

SECTION FIVE:

THE FORGIVENESS OF A FATHER

SECTION SIX:

THE PERSPECTIVE OF A FATHER

SECTION SEVEN:

☙ THE PROVISION OF A FATHER ❧

SECTION EIGHT:

☙ THE COMFORT OF A FATHER ❧

SECTION NINE:

☙ THE FELLOWSHIP OF A FATHER ❧

SECTION TEN:

❧ THE EMBRACE OF A FATHER ❧

Would you like to know God? Deeply? Intimately? Passionately? Would you like to know his thoughts, understand his feelings, see through his eyes? Although you can't know God physically, you can know what he is like; know the depths of his love; know what pleases him.

By looking at examples of everyday fathers who've demonstrated an aspect of God's virtues in uncommon ways, you can experience the father-heart of God.

The Heart of a Father will demonstrate God's nature by giving you well-defined examples of earthly fathers who have, in one way or another, exemplified God's character. These tangible stories, much like the teachings of Jesus, will show what God is like. These inspiring, eye-opening, heartfelt stories will guide you into a deeper relationship with God, the Father. Short enough to be read in one sitting, each story reveals a different aspect of God's nature.

For many people the image of God as Father isn't a pleasant one because the image of their earthly father wasn't pleasant. Some view fathers as distant, uninvolved, and uncaring persons. Others remember an evil man who molested them, physically and/or emotionally. Still others picture a strict disciplinarian who relentlessly pushed them, never offering words of encouragement or love.

Even at their best, fathers break promises, lose their tempers, and often fail. There are times, however, when a man rises above the commonplace and does something so extraordinary that it merits emulation. These are the moments and the times we will share with you in *The Heart of a Father*.

Many books have been written on the subject of God as Father. Few have dared to demonstrate God's nature by comparing the positive attributes of earthly fathers to the nature of God. Yet that is exactly what Jesus taught us to do in the Lord's Prayer when he addressed God as "Our Father."

In all areas and in all ways God *is* an exalted Father. And in the pages of this book not only will God be exalted but you will come away with a deeper knowledge and intimacy of God, *your* Father.

Yes! You can know God!

The UNCONDITIONAL LOVE OF A FATHER

THE REUNION

MAX LUCADO

from *In the Grip of Grace*

A few weeks ago I traveled to the Midwest to pick up my two oldest daughters. They'd spent a week at camp. This wasn't their first time at camp, but it was their first time so far from home. The camp was great and the activities outstanding, but their hearts were heavy. They missed their mom and dad. And Mom and Dad weren't doing so well either.

Not wanting to risk any delayed flights, I flew up a day early. Parents weren't allowed to see their kids until 5:00 P.M., so I enjoyed the area, visited a few sights, and kept an eye on the time. My purpose wasn't to sightsee. My purpose was my kids.

I arrived at the camp at 3:00 P.M. A rope was stretched across the dirt road, and a sign dangling from the rope reminded me, "Parents may not enter until 5:00 P.M."

I wasn't alone at the rope. Other parents were already present. There was a lot of glancing at wristwatches. No in-depth conversations, just the expected "How are you?" "Where are you from?" and "How many kids?" Nothing much beyond that. Our minds were down that dirt road. At about 4:30, I noticed a few dads positioning themselves near the rope. Not to be outdone, I did the same. Though most of the slots were taken, there was room for one more parent. I squeezed past one mother who was unaware that the horses had been called to the track. I felt sorry for her, but not enough to give her my spot.

With five minutes to go, conversation ended. No more playing games; this was serious stuff. The cars were on the track. The runners were in the blocks. The countdown was on. All we needed was someone to lower the rope.

Two camp counselors appeared to perform the honors. They knew better than to take one end of the rope and cross the road to allow the parents to enter. Such a move would have been fatal; they wouldn't have survived the stampede. Rather than endanger their lives, each took one end of the rope and, on a prearranged signal, lowered it to the ground. (They had done this before.)

We were off!

I was ready for this moment. I had waited long enough. I began with a brisk walk, but out of the corner of my eye I saw a dad starting to trot. *So that's what it's going to take, eh?* Good thing I was wearing jogging shoes. I broke into a run. Enough preliminaries. The hour had struck and the rope was down, and I was willing to do what it took to see my kids.

God feels the same.

God is ready to see his own. He, too, is separated from his children. He, too, will do whatever is necessary to take them home. Yet, his desire leaves ours in the dust. Forget plane trips and rental cars: we're talking incarnation and sacrifice. Forget a night in a hotel; how about a lifetime on earth! I went from the state of Texas to the state of Missouri. He went from the state of being worshiped in heaven to being a baby in Bethlehem.

Why? He knows his children are without their father. And he knows we are powerless to return without his help.

"Andrea! Jenna! I'm here!" I shouted as I ran down the camp road. (I won the race.) I spotted Andrea first. She was under a canopy preparing to practice gymnastics. I called her name again. "Daddy!" she yelled and jumped into my arms.

There was no guarantee she'd respond. Though I had flown a thousand miles, rented a car, and waited an hour, she could have seen me and—heaven forbid!—ignored me. Some kids are too grown up to run to their parent in front of their friends.

But then there are those who have had enough camp food and

mosquito repellent to make them jump for joy at the sight of their father. Such was the case with Andrea.

All of a sudden, Andrea had gone from feeling homesick to feeling happy. Why? Only one difference. Her father had come to take her home.

TRUANT TEARS

C. VERNON HOSTETLER

I drove my fifteen-year-old son, Bob, to his Reading, Ohio, high school, and dropped him off at 7:30 A.M., as I had done every day for months. I knew the bell would ring at 7:37, signaling the beginning of another school day; I did not know that he would not be there when it did.

There was no one else to take him to school, no one else to fix him breakfast, or help with his homework, or earn a living to keep him in Converse shoes and bell bottoms. Bob's two older brothers had each left home for college, and his mother—my wife of twenty-seven years—had died of cancer the previous September, at age forty-nine. Within a few months of her funeral, I had lost my job, and Bob and I moved to a new neighborhood, where he enrolled in a new school and I commenced a new job as a traveling representative for a nonprofit organization.

So that morning, like every morning, I watched my son trudge alone through the crowd of teenagers that milled about in front of the school, and waited until he disappeared through the entrance before driving off. He was miserable; I knew that he had few friends at school, he was failing every class, and he had been caught skipping school more than once—but I didn't know how to help him.

As I often did, I stopped at a local Perkins Restaurant for coffee and pancakes and checked my appointments for the day. As I did this, I realized I had left important paper work at home. I drained the last swallow of coffee, left a tip, and paid my bill. Then I got into my 1974 Plymouth Duster and headed home.

When I arrived, I was surprised to find the front door unlocked. I was sure I had locked it when Bob and I left that morning. When I stepped into the living room, however, I received another surprise: Bob was sitting there. He was skipping school. He had gotten out of my car that morning and walked the two miles home as soon as I was out of sight. He had been willfully disobedient. Anger immediately rose in me, and I began to ponder what punishment I would dispense.

But Bob had not seen me enter. His eyes were closed. He wore a set of stereo headphones. He sat in an upholstered chair that had belonged to his mother. I saw by the record sleeve on the floor at his feet that he was listening to one of his mother's records, a selection of classical piano pieces (she herself had been an accomplished pianist). And a steady stream of tears coursed down his cheeks.

In an instant my anger evaporated. The son who sat before me was a truant, but he was also a boy who had lost his mother—as I had lost a wife. I knew that, of course, but his tears reminded me.

He still had not seen me. He didn't even know I was in the room. I sat down on the couch opposite him. And when he finally opened his eyes, tears were streaming down my cheeks too.

I don't recall what else I did that day in response to my son's truancy. But I will always remember the moment when God touched my heart and united my grief and my son's in a union of compassion and comfort.

"LONGER, DADDY, LONGER..."

GARY SMALLEY
JOHN TRENT, PH.D.

from *Leaving the Light On*

Recently a woman grabbed my arm at a conference after I (John) had finished speaking on the enormous need we all have for affirmation.

"Dr. Trent, may I tell you my story?" she asked. "Actually, it's a story of something my son did with my granddaughter that illustrates what you've been talking about—the importance of affirmation.

"My son has two daughters, one who's five and one who is in the 'terrible twos.'" When a *grandmother* says this child is in the "terrible twos," *believe me*, she is!

"For several years my son has taken the oldest girl out for a 'date' time, but he had never taken the two-year-old until recently. On his first 'date' with the younger one, he took her out for breakfast at a local fast food restaurant.

"They had just gotten their pancakes and my son decided it would be a good time to tell this child how much he loved and appreciated her."

"Jenny," her son had said, "I want you to know how much I love you, and how special you are to Mom and me. We prayed for you for years, and now that you're here and growing up to be such a wonderful girl, we couldn't be more proud of you."

Once he had said all this, he stopped talking and reached over for his fork to begin eating . . . but he never got the fork to his mouth.

His daughter reached out her little hand and laid it on her father's hand. His eyes went to hers, and in a soft, pleading voice she said, *"Longer, Daddy, longer . . ."*

He put his fork down and proceeded to tell her some more reasons and ways they loved and appreciated her, and then he again reached for his fork. A second time . . . and a third . . . and a fourth time he heard the words, "Longer, Daddy, longer . . ."

This father never did get much to eat that morning, but his daughter got the emotional nourishment she needed so much. In fact, a few days later, she spontaneously ran up to her mother and said, "I'm a really special daughter, Mommy. Daddy told me so."

I WAS ON HIS MIND

MICHAEL J. MASSIE

I remember the maroon carpet that covered the basement steps in my parents' house on Andrew Avenue. My father used to spend countless hours with my sister and me playing on that carpet. A great deal of our playtime was in the basement or on those stairs. We would shoot down plastic cowboys and Indians with rubber bands, wrestle, and play hide-and-seek. I struggle now to remember the actual dimensions of our basement, but I will never forget the carpet, because it was on that carpet that my father demonstrated how much he loved his children by spending hours with us.

On December 28, 1981, my sister and I were in the basement playing with our new Christmas toys when we heard a "thud" from upstairs. Something was going on in the kitchen above our heads. I sensed that something was not quite right.

Normally, large "thuds" came from my sister and me knocking each other over. Usually our roughhousing was followed by choruses of blaming each other, and then one of us would spend some time in our room as punishment.

After a few minutes of silence from upstairs, my mother opened the basement door and called in a strained voice, "Mike, Devon, come up here for a minute."

"Why, Mom?" we replied in our typical childhood manner.

"Your dad wants to see you," she answered.

My sister and I raced to the top of the steps, but as we clambered through the basement doorway we were greeted with an unusual sight. Our father was lying on his back, staring blankly at the ceiling.

Dad reached out in our direction with one arm. "Come here and let me give you both a hug."

I had never seen my father in such a helpless position. His left arm lay next to his side, while he blindly gestured with his right arm for us to come to him. His words were calming, but nothing could keep down the panic that rose within my stomach as tears leapt to my eyes. Underneath his calm words was the pain of uncertainty. He hugged my sister and me individually with one arm, not with the strength of his usual bear hugs.

His voice shook as he told us, "Everything will be okay. Listen to and obey your mother. I am going away for a while."

Without any further explanation my mother shuffled us back into the basement, and the door was closed solidly behind us. We were supposed to go back into the basement and resume playing. I'm sure my mother and father thought they were protecting us from some emotional harm, but neither one of us made it back down the steps. Instead, we sat by the door, huddled together with our faces on the maroon carpet, watching everything we could see through the crack at the bottom of the door.

It was the first time my sister and I actually sat quietly together without causing a fuss. Something serious was taking place. The thought of our father as blind, crippled, and maybe dying scared us. The only comfort we had was in each other and the familiar maroon carpet, which had been the playground upon which our father launched countless adventures.

As the lights from the ambulance reflected off the eggshell white walls, the feet of the EMTs walked past to check on our motionless father. As they wheeled in the stretcher, their muffled words penetrated the basement door. "Call ahead to the hospital . . ."

We watched and we waited. I had no answers for my younger sister's questions. When all was quiet, we retreated down the steps. After a short time my mother came downstairs and held us as we all cried. Fear and pain wracked my mother's voice as she explained, "Your father is very sick, and he had to go to the hospital, but he will be all right."

Several days later my sister and I were allowed to visit my father at the hospital. He grinned as we walked into the room. He was regaining some strength, but he was going to be in the hospital for quite some time. Through the next several weeks friends and relatives visited to lend their support, but the important part is that eventually Dad came home.

Over the years I have pieced together bits of information about what really happened that night. My father suffered from what doctors would later call a stroke. Dad refers to it as the day his "brain blew up." My father not only recovered, but his only side effect was the loss of a quarter of his eyesight. The blindness in the upper left-hand corners of his eyes is his constant reminder that he must rely on God to see things clearly. Dad memorized 1 Corinthians 13:12 to help him remember God's strength: "Now we see but a poor reflection as in a mirror; then we shall see face to face."

After the stroke, my father traveled to several churches in our hometown to give his testimony—his biggest audiences were youth groups. On one occasion, when I was around the age of thirteen, I had the opportunity to go with my father and listen to his message. Until then I believed I'd heard all about how God had healed and continued to heal my father, but there was a part of his testimony that I had never heard before. It was a part that would change me spiritually—a part that would help me understand what it meant for God to love me unconditionally.

"As I lay on the floor, completely blind and not able to feel half of my body, I told my wife I wanted to see my children one last time. I was sure I was dying, but the irony was that even if my children had been right next to me, I wouldn't have been able to see them. My wife called Mike and Devon upstairs, and I placed my good arm around each of them in turn and told them I loved them. I told them not to worry, that everything would be okay. Then I sent them back downstairs, not wanting to worry them. The ambulance arrived, and I was loaded into the back.

"At this point everyone wonders what you would say to God. Do you pray for the pain to stop? Do you pray for a quick death so that you can be with the Lord? Do you pray to be healed instantly? I found myself praying the one thing that came to mind: 'Lord, when I die, don't let my children be bitter.' The most important thing for me at the time when I thought I was dying was that my children not grow to hate the God I loved so much."

My father continued to give the rest of his testimony, but I could hear nothing else. I never knew that my father's *last* thoughts as they were taking him away were of my little sister and me. I began to weep as I fully realized how unworthy I was of so great a love. I did nothing to deserve my father's love, and yet he gave it so freely that he was thinking of me while he thought he was dying.

When they put my dad into the back of that ambulance, he exhibited the unconditional love of God the Almighty. His only concern was for his children, no matter the pain, the suffering, and the proximity of death. Every time I see my father, I am reminded in some way of the unconditional love and grace that my heavenly Father has given to me. No matter what the cost, I know that God loves me. I know this because my dad showed me what unconditional love was all about.

Unconditional love remembers nothing of your past mistakes. It does not look for worthiness. Unconditional love picks up the imperfect child in a large embrace. Unconditional love says, "My thoughts are of you always, and I want you to be my child." My dad wanted nothing less than the best for his children, no matter our past or future mistakes. He wanted us to love God and to experience his love.

My heavenly Father wants the best for all his children. He wants us to love him and experience his love. My heavenly Father's unconditional love helps me to know that when my dad does leave this world, I will not be bitter.

FATHER-IN-LAW LOVE

LINDA KNIGHT

The sun is usually warm on a summer's day in southern Ontario, but today the breeze is cool and the skies are gray and shadowy and dark like the mist that covers my soul.

My husband has been laid off for over two months. *Laid off* is such a cruel word. It carries a sting with it, like a spear tipped with half-truths and poisons.

I put our toddler in his stroller as our two other young sons join me. Maybe a walk to the local park will help brighten my lagging spirits. I smile as the boys laugh and scamper along happily, oblivious to the stacks of bills piling up, the taxes that are overdue, and the cupboards that are growing more and more sparse. For a few hours, however, we forget all of that and simply revel in each other's company.

We lie on the grass and study the clouds, naming the shapes that catch our attention. We sing our favorite nursery songs, play catch, practice our somersaults, and just have fun.

We spread our blanket on the ground, bow our heads, and sing our mealtime grace to God. Aaron, our five-year-old, asks God to help his daddy find a job. I quickly look away so they won't see the tears wetting my cheeks as my thoughts echo Aaron's prayer, *Yes, God, please help Daddy find a job.*

We pack up our belongings and head back home to find my father-in-law of fifteen years waiting for us. I sense a deep caring in the creases of his smile as he opens his arms wide to welcome the boys. He goes to his car to unload bags of groceries.

I hear him speak, and his gentle voice is like a thousand prayers suddenly answered. This humble man who has worked so hard since he was thirteen, presses money into my trembling hands.

"Take it," he insists. "Take it. I want to help."

Much time has passed since then, and the boys have all grown. Life has become a procession of births and deaths and tears and smiles, and the gentle remembrance of a father-in-law's love.

SEE YOU AT THE HOUSE

BOB BENSON

from *See You at the House*

> *The one who calls you is faithful and he will do it.*
> —1 Thessalonians 5:24

For a long time when it was halftime at football games, I wished the bands would finish and get off the field so we could get back to watching the real action. A time came, however, when I could hardly wait for the half to be over so the field would be cleared of ball players and referees. Now the main event would begin! Patrick had joined the band.

When our youngest son joined the high school band, he introduced us to a world we had not even known existed as we followed our other four through this period of their lives. We learned that "band-itry," like most everything else Americans do, was a subculture all its own. It has its own rules, regulations, contests, performances, championships, trophies, winners, losers, pageantry, intricate marching patterns, and exciting music.

At Patrick's school, the Marching Cougars would begin their season the first week in August with a six-day camp of rigorous drill and rehearsal to learn the show for the coming season. The director had already spent the first two months of the summer working on the musical arrangements and the drill itself. We always looked forward to the last day of camp, for there was an exciting (although ragged) first performance for the parents.

Every weekday afternoon for the rest of August the band was on the practice field polishing the music and marching steps. Early in September the performances would begin at the Friday night football games both at home and away. There were also contests and band festivals on Saturdays, which were all part of the process leading up to the third Saturday in October when the Class A State Championship was held.

The climactic afternoon and evening of the state championship was a colorful panorama of bands, parents, hot dogs, music, buses, nachos, an occasional dog on the field, and the all-time All-American pastime, competition. Beginning promptly at 1:00 P.M. and every twelfth minute thereafter, there was a band of trained, excited, nervous, talented kids lined up on the far side of the field awaiting the voice of the announcer over the loudspeaker: "Field Commander, is your band ready?" This inquiry was answered by the major or majorettes in an unbelievable set of motions, gyrations, and leaps that transformed the tipping of the hat and the nodding of the head into a ten-second extravaganza in itself. The announcer, over the roar of the crowd, a roar most often led by the majorette's mother and father, acknowledged this magnificent salute to readiness with the words that have been anticipated since the first moments of rehearsal camp, "You may begin."

In the next eight minutes (playing too long lowers the score), all of the hours of rehearsal and drill are put on the line. Late in the afternoon, the six finalists are announced and after a break for supper and for the spectators to get warm, the stands fill up again and the final competition begins for the trophies—First Place and the Governor's Cup. Each of the six bands repeats its performances but this time with the excitement and confidence of being in the finals and with the hope now of being number one. The good directors, like Mr. Van Dyke, had saved a wrinkle or two for the finals. The faces in the percussion section were painted, one side blue and one side white.

When the bands have finished and the judges are finally ready to make their decisions known, the six bands are standing in a row in formation on the field. And the loudspeakers blare forth, "The number six band with a score of 84.5 is . . . the number five band is . . . number four . . . three. . . ." And a great roar goes up when the name of the number two band is sounded forth. A tremendous roar that drowns out the cheers for Number Two because the only band left unnamed, and its rooting section of parents and friends, has suddenly realized that there is nobody else left between them and the championship. They are Number One!

It is a moment of almost unbearable pride and excitement if your kid is one of the members of the band they are naming when they say, "And the number one band in the state with a score of 94.5 is. . . ." Three years in a row Patrick and the Marching Cougars were the band in which the delirious bedlam broke out. There was another year when some three-quarters of a point taught them the agony of defeat.

The high point of a band's performance is the closer, or push, as Patrick's director called it. Usually it begins with the band close to the stands playing their final song. The intricate patterns have been marched and the percussion break has been played—and the band is in tight formation. There is a section of the music that is played softly and the band marches away, backs to the crowd. Then they wheel and march toward the stands playing full volume for the finale. It is called "blowing to the box" because the band gives the judges everything they have.

I asked Patrick if he could describe what it was like marching toward the stands filled with cheering parents and friends, playing wide open with all that paint on his face and finally coming to attention as the last echoes of the music of the concluding song of the final show are lost in the noise of the crowd. He grinned as if it were impossible to explain. I told him that if he thought it was exciting on the field he should just wait until a day somewhere, sometime when he was a dad at a state championship. And then he would see his kid turn and march toward him in perfect step with a hundred other kids, his head high and his back straight, beating fifty pounds of drums as if it were his task to set the tempo for the whole world. I told him if I was still around, I wanted to be sitting there with him. And then we can talk about what thrilling *really* is.

My thinking about this nudged me into some further thoughts about the heavenly Father. This One who is calling us. We all tend to believe (or at least fear) that the God who calls us is watching us. It makes all the difference in the world where we think he is sitting. As long as we think of him as the judge in the press box who is checking for smudges on our white shoes, for the misplayed notes, for marching out of step, for our hats falling off or any one of a dozen other things that can happen to us in performance, it is hard to keep from living our whole lives in fear of a button coming off our tunics.

It was Jesus himself who reminded us that we were to call him Father—"Abba, Father"—which is a lot more like calling him Dad. I think Jesus was telling us that our Father is the one in the stands who is standing on the seat, waving his coat in a circle over his head, with tears of pride and happiness running down his face.

SECTION *two*

The WISDOM
OF A FATHER

FLOUNDERING WITH MY FATHER

CHARLES R. SWINDOLL

from *Come Before Winter . . . and Share My Hope*

Floundering with my father is among my most cherished childhood memories.

Armed with a beat-up Coleman lantern, two gigs, a stringer . . . and clothed in old sneakers, faded jeans, torn shirts, and funny hats, we'd get to the water. When the sky got nice 'n' dark, we'd wade in. Not too far out, you understand, knee-deep was plenty. And off we'd stumble into the night to stab a few flat, brown creatures who chose our shoreline as the place for a shrimp supper.

Actually, my dad was more addicted to floundering than I. He went to get the fish. I went to be with him, which was fine for a while. By and by we'd round the point about a mile away from the bay cottage where the other members of the Swindoll tribe were. If we stopped and listened, we could hear them laughing like crazy. And here I was knee-deep in muddy, cold salt water . . . with nothing but thick darkness in front of me.

To this day I still remember looking back wistfully over my shoulder toward that ever-so-tiny light at the cabin in the distance. A few steps further and it was out of sight. No light, no more sounds of laughter, just the glow of a lantern and the reassuring words of my dad, who somehow knew the fears of a little boy walking in darkness next to him.

Soon I began asking myself why. Why in the world had I agreed to come? Why didn't I stay back with the family? And how long? If I asked him once, I must have asked a dozen times, "How much longer, Daddy? When are we gonna turn around?" In tones that were mellow and quiet, he comforted me. I asked, "What if the mantle burns out?" We brought along a flashlight. "What if the batteries are dead?" He was very familiar with the path that would get us back. While he was searching for flounder, I was looking and listening for relief . . . those marvelous words, "Well, Son, this is far enough. Let's turn around."

Instantly, I found myself wading on tiptoes, caring nothing about finding some poor flounder—only that light, that tiny signal in the distance that assured me my dad really knew the way. Once it was spotted, my entire personality changed. My anxieties were relieved. My questions were answered. Hope lit the darkness like a thousand lanterns . . . thanks to one tiny light at the end of my childhood tunnel of fears.

Four long decades have passed since I trudged through the darkness with my father, but they have not erased from my mind the incredible importance of hope. Its significance seems larger than life to me today. How powerful is its presence!

Take from us our wealth and we are hindered. Take our health and we are handicapped. Take our purpose and we are slowed, temporarily confused. But take away our hope and we are plunged into deepest darkness . . . stopped dead in our tracks, paralyzed. Wondering, "Why?" Asking, "How much longer? Will this cold, dark winter ever end? Does He know where I am?"

Then the Father says, "That's far enough," and how sweet it is! Like blooms through melting snow, long-awaited color returns to our life. The stream, once frozen hard, starts to thaw. Hope revives and washes over us.

There is nothing like light, however small and distant, to put us on tiptoes in the darkness. Our whole personality changes when our Father utters those magical words, "Let's turn around!" His promises suddenly gain substance as reassuring hope warms us like the sun in late March.

Inevitably, spring follows winter. Every year. Yes, including this one. Barren days, like naked limbs, will soon be clothed with fresh life. Do you need that reminder today? Are you ready for some sunshine on your shoulders . . . a few green sprouts poking up through all that white? A light at the end of your tunnel?

Look! There it is in the distance. It may be tiny, but it's there. You made it! Your Father knew exactly where He was going. And why. And for how long. That cottage in the distance? Let's name it New Hope. You'll soon be there, laughing again with the family.

You may live to see the day when your journey into the darkness is among your most cherished memories.

TRUST HIM

JONI EARECKSON
WITH JOE MUSSER

from *Joni*

I withdrew into myself and the solitude of home. After being away so long, I appreciated the old house with all its pleasant memories. Yet for some reason, I couldn't really feel at home there anymore; I felt awkward in my own home.

This left me with eerie, anxious feelings like the depression I felt trying to adjust during those nightmarish months after my accident.

"What's the matter, honey?" Dad finally asked.

"I—I don't know, Daddy. I'm just sad—depressed."

Dad nodded.

"I don't know if I can ever really adjust to being paralyzed," I told him. "Just when I think I've got things under control, I go into a tailspin."

"Well, you just take your time, Joni. We'll do anything—anything at all to help, you know that." His sparkling blue eyes and smiling face radiated love and encouragement.

I sighed deeply, then said, "I guess the thing that affects me most is that I'm so helpless. I look around the house here, and everywhere I look I see the things you've built and created. It's really sad to think that I can't leave a legacy like you. When you're gone, you will have left us with beautiful buildings, paintings, sculpture, art. Even the furniture you've made. I can never do any of that. I can never leave a legacy—"

Dad wrinkled his forehead for a moment, then grinned again. "You've got it all wrong. These things I've done with my hands don't mean anything. It's more important that you build character. Leave something of yourself behind. Y'see? You don't build character with your hands."

"Maybe you're right, Daddy."

"Of course I am."

"But why does God allow all this? Look at our family. We've had more than our share of heartbreak—first my accident, then Jay's divorce, now—now little Kelly (my niece dying of brain cancer). It's so unfair," I cried.

Daddy put his hands on my shoulders and looked straight into my eyes. "Maybe we'll never know the 'why' of our troubles, Joni. Look—I'm not a minister or a writer—I don't know exactly how to describe what's happening to us. But, Joni, I have to believe God knows what He's doing."

"I don't know," I offered.

"Look, how many times have you heard somebody—we've done it ourselves many times—pray piously: 'Lord, I'm such a sinner. I deserve hell and Your worst condemnation. Thank You for saving me.' We tell God in one breath that we aren't worthy of His goodness. Then, if we happen to run into some trouble or suffering, we get bitter and cry out against God: 'Lord, what are You doing to me?!' Y'see? I think that if we admit we deserve the worst—hell—and then only get a taste of it by having to suffer, we ought to try somehow to live with it, don't you?"

"Do you think I deserved to be paralyzed—that God is punishing me?"

"Of course not, honey. That was taken care of on the cross. I can't say why He allowed this to happen. But I have to believe He knows what He's doing. Trust Him, Joni. Trust Him."

HE ALLOWS ME
TO HUNGER

AMY CARMICHAEL

from *His Thoughts Said . . . His Father Said*

O God, you are my God, earnestly I seek you; my soul thirsts for you, my body longs for you, in a dry and weary land where there is no water . . .

   My soul will be satisfied as with the richest of foods; with singing lips my mouth will praise you. —Psalm 63:1, 5

The son found himself in a barren place.

His Father said, "In *this* place I will give you the peace you are longing for. *Here* I will give you spiritual food that will nourish you. You are always with Me—no matter what the circumstances—and all that I have is yours."

Then the Father, with great gentleness, drew the son to himself. Quietly, He said, "I am the one who allowed you to come into these humbling circumstances, and allowed you to hunger. I did this so that I might feed you with *manna*—My bread from heaven!

"Only in this way could I help you to know that you cannot live by bread alone, but by every word that proceeds from *My* mouth."

The son said, "Give me this bread always!"

And when he grew thirsty he learned to cry . . . "The light of your face is my life!"

. . . Later still, the son wondered why one like himself, who is so richly fed and cared for at times, should at other times feel so poor and needy and thirsty.

His Father replied by asking four questions:

"Can someone who has never thirsted know how precious is My living water?

"Can someone who has never discovered rivers of these living waters flowing on barren heights—can he ever lead his thirsty friend to those rivers?

"Can someone who has never walked the deep valleys of the spirit help a friend who is fainting—or lead this friend to the wellsprings that will save the life of his soul?

"Can someone who has never seen burning sands in the wilderness turn into a refreshing pool—can he speak in praise of My marvels, or My power?"

My Father, I've been struggling within, because of some of the places life has led me . . . and struggling with you, too. . . .

I come to you today, Father, and ask you to begin refreshing and nourishing my soul again.

"WHAT ARE YOU GOING TO DO ABOUT IT?"

BOB BENSON

from *See You at the House*

The family is just about the place that I want to succeed the most. In fact, I feel that if I fail here, my life will be a failure in spite of everything else that I accomplish, and if I can succeed here, it will somehow atone for all the other failures of my whole life. My most often and fervent prayer is that I will be a successful father.

I love to sing the song that goes, "I have decided to follow Jesus, no turning back, no turning back." And I like the second verse, "Take this world but give me Jesus, no turning back, no turning back." But when they come to the last verse, I have to drop out because I cannot sing, "Though none go with me still I will follow, no turning back, no turning back."

I can't sing it. If I live my life in such a way that I must go by myself, then I think I feel like Moses must have felt when he told the Lord, "If the children don't get to go to Canaan, then blot my name out of the book, too."

I was reading somewhere of a retreat for career men and, at the end of the weekend, the last thing each man was to do was to write a headline that he would most like to see in the newspaper about himself. One man wrote, "Henry Smith Was Elected Father of the Year Today—His Wife and Family Were the Judges." But everyone doesn't feel this way. I have actually talked to parents who say that it never occurred to them to tell their children that they loved them. I think that some of the most effective things that I have ever done in retreats and conferences was to send people back home to express love to their kids.

I am a firm believer that the only way to even try to be a parent is with the use of the power of love. We have tried a variety of ways of disciplining our children. When they were small enough, we would give them a quick swat on the rear end. There were times when I felt that all the nerve endings that had to do with hearing, quietness, muscle control, and other vital signs were centered in that general area of the body where they sat down. And I must admit that there were times when I felt that it worked. We used to have a Volkswagen, and when things weren't going right in the backseat, you could backhand everybody including Peggy with one stroke of your arm. I was the biggest and they couldn't hit me back, or if they did it was only on the kneecap and didn't hurt too much.

But then they got bigger. I used to wrestle Robert and Mike, and then Mike and I used to wrestle Robert. I try not to wrestle with any of them now. If I wanted to discipline Mike today by paddling him, I would have to say, "Mike, sir, how would you like to bend over so that I can bring you into line?" Because when he is standing up straight he is taller than I am.

When the older boys hit the teens we tried grounding them once or twice. You know, "You can't leave the yard all weekend except to go to church." I don't know who gets the worst end of that deal—the "groun-dee" or the "groundor." I just know it doesn't make for much of a weekend with an unhappy boy or two sitting around. And it really doesn't work because if they are old enough and mad enough, they will just leave home.

And you can cut off their allowance but who needs two dollars a week anyway. So what do you do—ignore them, just keep your head in the newspaper until they get a haircut—what do you do? I believe that the most powerful step you can take is to turn the fervor of your love up another ten degrees.

It has been my intention as a parent to believe in and respect the specialness of the calling of God in the hearts and lives of my children. I think I can accurately be described as a "nondirective" parent. I'm not sure that this is always necessarily best—and I'm not sure altogether how I came to be this way. Part of the reason is my natural readiness to avoid confrontation if I can. Part of the reason is that I want to believe everything will work out for everybody.

Then, I think, too, that I got caught in the way the generations swing back and forth in their manner of parenting. I remember one day when my dad and I were walking along on Church Street in front of Harvey's Department Store in Nashville. I noticed a plaque in the sidewalk which noted the paving had been done in 1927, and I asked Dad if he had walked over this same spot with his father in days gone by. He said he didn't think so. Because he had been the last child in a large family, he had always felt his dad was tired of children by the time he came along. So he didn't remember their walking many places together. Thinking that his father had not been as prominent in his life as he would have liked for him to have been, my dad decided early on that he would get involved in the lives of his children.

For instance, he was an expert at knowing things like where you were supposed to go to college. I didn't have to spend a lot of time deliberating where to pursue my education after high school. Quite simply, I went to the place where he was sending the tuition money. I graduated from high school one night at 8:00 and caught the 10:30 bus. The next morning I was 220 miles away in freshman Greek class at Asbury College. As I said, my dad got involved in the lives and decisions of his children.

Maybe this accounts in some measure for my hanging back and encouraging my five to make up their own minds. One of them will come to me and say, "What should I do about this?" And I will try to look as wise as I can. I will pause significantly, as fathers will do, indicating that I am deep in thought about the matter. Then I make a studied and weighty pronouncement. Most of the time I profoundly answer, "I dunno."

I am not at all convinced that this is a superior way of parenting. Already some of my sons are old enough to look back and point to given moments in their lives when they needed more direction than their father was able or willing to provide. But I have earnestly believed, and tried to get my children to believe, that if they listened to the quiet voice within they would know the answer, because a part of his image within them is his calling voice.

Not too terribly long ago, there were some rumors that Mike was in some trouble. First they came from school and then, of course, they grew more rampant in the fertile soil of the church. And so we called a family council for Peg and I. "What are you going to do about it?" she said.

"Well, what are you going to do about it?" was my reply. "Will we confront him and ask him about it? Will we assume he didn't and treat him like he did? Will we accuse him? Will we subtly tighten the reins of his freedom until he 'cracks' and it becomes evident as to the truth of the rumors?"

Now to be sure, Peg is more of the "Let's get this all out in the open" type and I, through my natural wisdom, intelligence, and cowardice, am generally willing and able to run from all the confrontations, crises, and summit meetings that I can. Unfortunately, this time she chose to defer to me as the leader of the home and turned the matter over to me. With only a couple more questions.

"What are you going to do if it's *not* true?"

"I'm going to continue to go into his room at night and kneel by his bed and I am going to rub his back for a moment (he sleeps on his stomach) and say, 'Mike, I love you and I am proud to be your dad. I hope you sleep well and I'll see you in the morning. Goodnight.' "

"And what are you going to do if it *is* true?"

"I'm going to continue to go into his room at night and kneel by his bed and I am going to rub his back for a moment (he sleeps on his stomach) and say, 'Mike, I love you and I am proud to be your dad. I hope you sleep well and I'll see you in the morning. Goodnight.' "

It was a couple of months later that he came, first to his mom, and then later to me, and said, "I was in some trouble at school but I got it worked out. I'm sorry as I can be and it won't happen again." And we were doubly proud the day that Mike wrote home from school, "Send me my Bible, I am running for freshman class chaplain." We did and he was.

I really do believe that steady, patient, unceasing, deep, expressed, *oozed* love is the only reliable option open to parents. It's better than advice, grounding, cutting the allowance, paddlings, punishments, threats, or any of the other dozens of dodges and ruses we work on our unsuspecting and waiting children. Just care, just love, just show it. *Do something.*

There have been some times when the temptation as a father has been to assume that it would be best to just go ahead and tell my children what they should do. Still, there was something that kept me from doing this. Maybe it was because I always somehow knew that I could not necessarily know what was right for a given child.

All of your children live in the same house and they ride in the same car and eat the same cereal for breakfast. They sometimes even wear the same hand-me-down tennis shoes. Your children have the same last name and the same parents. But your children are not the same. Not at all. Each one is unique. There are no "boiler plate" clauses that fit all children. They are like snowflakes with their own patterns and their own shapes and their own sizes. They have their own places to land. So their calling must come at precisely the right time and in the right way. They alone can hear the call of the One who can tell them what to be. And just because I am their parent, I cannot make them be tomatoes when they were destined to be radishes. Or scholars if they were meant to be farmers. Or accountants if what they really want is to become poets.

As a parent, I have decided that I can't do or decide or discern everything. But I can live like one who has heard the voice that called him. And I can love. And I can pray. And I can hope. And I can occasionally give advice. I can tell my children that there is a voice that will speak to them.

I can even drop hints. I can remind them (and have) that they could hear the inner voice better if they turned the stereo down, or better still, off altogether. I can say that the most important thing in life is to hear and obey the voice. And I can say that the gravest danger in all of life is to fail to hear and heed the voice.

But I cannot tell them what it will say to them. For the call that is within them is just to them.

NO BUSY SIGNALS HERE

GORDON MACDONALD

from *The Effective Father*

The effective father whose ear is open and whose wisdom makes him able to accept his children as they are, adds a final quality to his reputation for being approachable. Call it *flexible response*. To use another telephone analogy, he doesn't put his kids on "hold."

It was the middle of the night when Kris called my name. I heard her first "Daddy!" immediately and sprang out of bed and down the hall to her room. She was in distress. There had been a bad dream, and Kris was having a rough time sorting out what was real and what was part of the dream.

Why had she called her father? Because her instinct somehow told her that when equilibrium is in jeopardy, fathers can help restore balance. Her young mind had set a pattern of response to uneasy situations: call for Dad; he knows how to make upside-down things turn right-side up again. So in obedience to pattern she calls, and I come.

Suppose that I choose to belittle the "dumb dream." Suppose I yell down the hall, "What do you want?" When the report comes back that she is upset over a dream, suppose I respond with, "Don't worry about it! Everything will be all right; go back to sleep."

What do I really say? Perhaps I will seem to say, "Don't dump your problems on me; work them out for yourself. Your feelings are immature and stupid; make them dissolve. But by all means, leave me alone so that I can get some sleep."

But I don't do that; I have learned that *response* to my children when they are in crucial moments is of utmost importance. I go back to David and his sense of security and read his words, "I keep the Lord before me;

because he is at my right hand, I shall not be moved." Perhaps David had had some bad nocturnal moments and his father had come. Now as an adult he finds times in his life when everything seems like a bad dream. It is instinctive to cry out, and now it is not an earthly father who comes, but a heavenly Father who is constantly effective.

All effective fathers learn the importance of a wise and flexible response to their children's calls for attention. No busy signals here. No "hold" button.

Not long ago Gail and I heard the crash of breaking glass come from our living room. Running in the direction of the noise, we found our daughter behind a table where she was trying to retrieve a ball. Her foot had caught a cord, and a lamp—one both her mother and I prize—had fallen over. The globe of the lamp was in several pieces. Down deep within me was an impulse of immediate anger. I was ready to give vent to the anger because she had been playing ball in an area of the house where ball playing was out of bounds. She deserved—I thought—what my instincts prompted me to deliver.

But on the other hand, one look at her face told me that it was obvious that she knew she had been wrong. There she knelt, frozen, awaiting my response. I sensed that she was poised on the razor edge between trusting me with honest repentance or hardening into a defensive posture of excuses and passing the buck. My anger would provoke her to excuses; my understanding would give rise to her honest evaluation of her guilt.

Why is it hard to grant to children the same forgiveness we adults so desperately desire when we make mistakes? Must there be punishment for something that was done unintentionally—even if the initial act was actual disobedience? The anger dissolved, and I took her in my arms and hugged her. The tears flowed freely, and she expressed her sorrow. She now understood why we don't play ball games in the living room. But she understood something even more significant. I am approachable when she has made a bad mistake. In the future when the mistakes are even more dramatic, I want her to remember my response to the broken lamp. I want her to cry out my name instinctively, knowing that I am approachable and will respond flexibly in a mature assessment of the situation.

THE COLOR OF LOVE

JOSLYN GAINES VANDERPOOL

My father barely resembles the strong-framed man he once was. In recent years a series of devastating strokes has changed him. Despite his distorted speech and weakened body, what remains familiar is the sparkle in my father's eyes. While embracing him the other day, I desperately tried to hold on to all that he had taught me through the years. The memories and tears flowed as I remembered one lesson in particular my father had imparted.

In early 1967 my father retired from the U.S. Air Force and moved our family from the safe confines of a multi-cultural existence found in our old neighborhood to a non-integrated suburb. Midway in my second-grade year I started a new school. Besieged with the kind of trepidation of any child entering a new school, I clung to my father's hand as I was introduced to my teacher and the other children, none of whom resembled me in any way.

As the only African-American in the classroom, I felt intimidated by the whispers and stares of the other children. Before I was seated by my teacher, my father gave my hand one more long squeeze and left, looking back over his shoulder.

The day was pure torture. During recess my voice was silenced by name-calling, hushed laughter behind my back, and jokes about my skin color. I held steady though—no tears, just a warm sensation of discomfort rode up my spine. I wanted to leave, but the day dragged on.

Finally, when it was time to go, I was up with my books, ready to bolt. Before I reached the door, my teacher asked if anyone would walk me home. No one volunteered.

"I can get home on my own," I mumbled.

As I began to walk across a broad field, some boys—one in particular, with curly blond hair and a wiry stance—unleashed an onslaught of derogatory words aimed toward me. The "N" word was the most prominent in his angry barrage.

Fearing I would be beaten up, I ran home. I was certain to find an empty house with no one to greet me, because my sister would still be in school, and my parents both worked. Mercifully, as if God meant for him to be there, my father was home. I rushed to him, and he held me tightly with his strong arms.

Through tears and broken sentences, I told him what had happened. After listening intently, my father tried to soothe me.

"You aren't a nigger, sweetheart. Let me show you what the word *nigger* means," he said.

My father brought out the dictionary and read the definition of *nigger*, which at that time was termed a coward.

"The only coward was the boy who yelled at you. He called you names because of his own fears. You can't hate him for his ignorance. I feel sorry for him because he just doesn't know how special you are. We're all special in God's eyes, and our people are beautiful and strong no matter what anyone says. So let that boy and anybody else who calls you a name know that."

In essence, my father built my esteem and pride in myself and in my heritage. Without hate, anger, or fear in his words, he encouraged me to accept people for who they are without inflicting the kind of pain that had been directed toward me.

After that afternoon, some still taunted me, but now I had the gift of courage to sustain me through their attacks. The next time I was called a "nigger," "darkie," or "chocolate girl," I didn't run.

I turned around to the blond boy and remembered my father's words.

"I'm not a nigger!" I shouted, relieved that I had stood up for myself. "I'm special, just like you!"

Stunned by my reaction, the boy had no response. Even more amazing than my speaking up that day was the fact that the blond boy began walking me home after school.

One day as my newfound friend and I were heading home, another boy asked him angrily, "Why are you walking with that nigger?"

"She's not a nigger. She's my friend," he said simply.

Over the next few years, my school began to change as the community became more integrated. As children, we learned how to embrace as friends regardless of the color of our skin.

That day in 1967 will always burn brilliantly in my mind. I will never forget how the steadfast love and infinite wisdom of my father eased my pain. Although today my father's body may be more fragile, his gait less assured, and his words more difficult for him to express, what I treasure is the lesson he gave me long ago. Like the sparkle in his eyes, the words he spoke remain, guiding me through life.

SECTION *Three*

The DISCIPLINE
OF A FATHER

DADDY, MAKE HIM STOP!

WAYNE HOLMES

O nce I was with my children playing the game "Remember When." Fond recollections of precious times came to mind, but one in particular has remained. It exemplified the tough love parents must have for their children.

On that occasion, I had decided to build a play-set for the children. I settled on an elaborate system consisting of a platform, slide, sandbox, swings, overhead ladder, and a cargo net. In the course of construction, I made use of a double-sided thatching rake. Being pressed for time one evening, I left the rake outside while we went out to eat. Not having checked on my progress after school, when we arrived home from the restaurant, the kids wanted to have a look, even though it was already dark. Crystal and her brother Barcley jumped out of the car and ran into the backyard. Before we made it inside, Crystal returned. She looked up at me with a sad expression and calmly admonished me, "Dad, you should've put the rake away. If you had, I wouldn't have stepped on it."

She spoke so softly, I had no clue she was hurt. As she finished her sentence, the corners of her mouth turned down, and she started to cry.

"Crystal, let me look at your foot," I said.

Her toes were cut, and blood flowed freely. I rushed her inside. Her mother washed the toes, wrapped a cloth around them, and we drove Crystal to Children's Hospital, where she received immediate attention. The deep cuts required stitches.

"Daddy, stay with me," Crystal said, between her sobs. "Don't make me go in there alone."

With the doctor's approval, I consented, though I've never been comfortable with the sights, sounds, and smells that accompany a hospital room.

Going into the room was difficult enough, but the doctor insisted on my participation.

"Hold her while I give her a shot," he said.

Guilt and remorse attacked as I approached my little girl.

Dear God, what have I done? I prayed as I walked to the front of the table. *Not only have I caused my child to be hurt by not putting the rake away, but now I have to hold her down and make her suffer even more. Please help her, Lord—and help me too.*

I held Crystal's slender shoulders, hoping the ordeal would be over as quickly as possible. I also hoped that she would forgive me—not only for my negligence but also for my part in causing her even more suffering.

After enough time had elapsed for the painkiller to take effect, the doctor sewed, while I watched. A few stitches later, Crystal grabbed my arms with all her might and screamed loudly. Obviously the painkiller was having no effect and she felt the needle as it bored through her flesh. Surprised by Crystal's reaction, the doctor stopped sewing.

"The anesthesia must not have reached this area," the doctor said. "I'll have to give her another injection."

Crystal clutched me even tighter than before.

"Daddy, make him stop! Please, Daddy, don't let him hurt me," she begged.

A sense of helplessness flattened my spirit. My daughter was in severe pain and she looked to me to make it go away.

But I didn't make it go away! In fact, I even helped the doctor. My strong but quivering hands held my daughter firmly on the table, forcing her to let the doctor perform the surgery she needed.

I wasn't cruel to my daughter when I refused to intercede on her behalf. Though it broke my heart, and I wanted to make the doctor stop, what I allowed to happen was for her own good.

This painful scene with Crystal screaming and pleading was a little more than I could handle. Of course, I did my best to be there emotionally for her until the ordeal was over, but as soon as the doctor finished, a queasiness floated to the surface of my consciousness.

"Are you feeling all right?" the doctor asked me.

"I feel a little lightheaded."

"Lie down," he ordered.

I became the center of attention, and Crystal seemed to enjoy the sudden change of events as I lay flat on my back, embarrassed, and concerned about my perceived manliness. Crystal seemed to forget about the ordeal she had just gone through. She couldn't wait to see her mother to tell her, "Dad almost passed out." The whole family enjoyed a good laugh at my expense.

Playing the reminiscing game with my children that day gave me cause to reflect about some of the painful experiences in my own life. In the midst of situations that seemed too painful to live through, I've often cried out to my heavenly Father for help. "Please, dear God, make the pain go away! Make it stop!"

At times it's felt as if God not only permitted my pain but also held me down, forced me to suffer through it, and completely ignored my cries for help. The lesson I learned from Crystal teaches me that God does love me. If I am suffering, I can rest assured there is a reason for it.

At times I become angry at God for saying no to my hurts, and for his refusing to intervene on my behalf. Just as Crystal's pain was short-lived, so too is mine. Being able to laugh at her dad was certainly helpful, but even without my near fainting spell, the ordeal would've been forgiven and forgotten. She didn't accuse me or ask me why I didn't make the doctor stop. She trusted me—trusted that I had her best interest at heart.

From this experience I learned that God is not my enemy. If he says no, he has his reasons. If he holds me, forces me to feel the pain, then he holds me with hands of love. With a heart that embraces me he sees the pain I'm going through. Crying out to him—even screaming for him to stop—is normal and acceptable. But I need to go one step further, and, in childlike faith, put my trust in him. He is, after all, a better father than I'll ever be. He would never do anything that wasn't in my own best interest.

FAITH ON TWO WHEELS

FAYE NEFF

D o you sometimes feel that God is nowhere to be found? Your prayers seem to fall into a void. The Bible is lifeless, and worship is stale. God has disappeared, and you don't know why.

Don't be embarrassed. You're in good company. Job knew that lonely feeling. So did Isaiah, who cried out, "Truly, you are a God who hides himself, O God of Israel, the Savior" (Isaiah 45:15 NRSV). On the cross, even Jesus felt God-forsaken.

I sometimes feel the same way. I've never been stuck there for long, and that feeling always passes sooner or later. It feels long, however, while I'm groping in the dark for a God who can't be found.

There is much about this that I don't understand, but I have learned one thing. Just because I can't find God doesn't mean that God has left town. Even when he is invisible, God is still trustworthy. I learned this lesson from my father. Dad taught me to ride a bicycle, and at the same time he taught me about faith.

My first bicycle was a beautiful dream come true! Streamers flowed from the handle-grips, and chrome fenders shone like polished silver. Mounted on the butterfly handlebars were a battery-powered horn and a light for night riding.

Money was sometimes in short supply at our house, and my parents believed in buying things my brother and I could grow into. Winter coats had room enough for me and my dog. My blue jeans had such long legs that it took ten minutes each morning just to roll the cuffs. My shoes had so much toe room that I walked around like Beppo the Clown, my feet entering the room several seconds ahead of my chin.

So naturally my parents bought me a bicycle I could grow into. This bike was huge—the Paul Bunyan model—and it took me months to learn to ride it. I wasn't athletic, and this bicycle was more than I could handle. I crashed into trees, I fell in front of cars, I tumbled into ditches. Imagine what would have happened without the training wheels!

Sometimes after supper Dad came out to help. He'd hold on to the back of my banana seat and trot along behind me, holding me up. Every evening the conversation was the same:

"Don't let go!" I'd say. "Hang on until I'm going strong."

"Don't worry," Dad would reply, "I'll be right here as long as you need me."

From my perspective, there was one serious problem with this system. I couldn't see my father behind me. I was so shaky I didn't dare glance over my shoulder. Both eyes were focused on the street, so as I rode along I couldn't keep an eye on Dad back there.

All I could do was keep pedaling. I had to trust that Dad was behind me. I had to believe that he would do what he promised. I had to have faith that he would hold me up as long as I needed it.

Looking back, I realize now that Dad always did his part. I careened and wobbled, slipped off the pedals, fell off the seat, and hit every pothole, but Dad kept his grip. He kept his promise. On those evening rides, I discovered that I didn't have to see someone with my eyes in order to count on him with my heart.

That's how I learned that an unseen God can still be trusted. A hidden God is not an absent God. Even when we can't see him, God is still within arm's reach. Even when we can't get a grip on the Father, the Father keeps his grip on us.

I finally mastered the bicycling part of the lesson. On the trusting part, I still wobble sometimes. Life is a bumpy ride with bad brakes, especially when you feel all alone on the road. But wobbly or not, I don't have the urge to look over my shoulder as often these days. I just keep on pedaling and trusting. I hang on to the handlebars, and somewhere out of sight God hangs on to me.

LIFE IN WHITE WATER

GORDON MACDONALD

from *The Effective Father*

L et's talk about laws—at least a few of them. Take a regard for truthfulness, for example. Respect for truth is something that should be established at the very beginning of childhood. It was an issue that God said was important when he first confronted Israel with his plan of righteous living.

My youth was marked by the emphasis that my father placed upon telling the truth—whatever the consequences. In my earliest childhood, he made it plain that lying would be met with the severest of punishments. Truthfulness, on the other hand, would be enthusiastically affirmed. I soon found out that he meant what he said. It was better, I learned, to own up to bad behavior than to attempt to cover it up—Watergate style. He had a way of finding things out, and improper behavior compounded by lying was the ultimate in family crime at our house. If such an occasion arose, he threw the book at me. I'm glad he did.

My father did see this thing both ways, and he was equally diligent about accepting, affirming, and rewarding me when he knew that I had faced the truth, even when it was painful.

By the age of five or six, truth telling had become an automatic thing. I remember the day when the observance of this basic rule of family conduct really paid off. Someone had set the underbrush on fire in an empty lot near our home. Before long the firemen arrived with their hoses and went to work. Right behind them were the police with their questions. Someone pointed the finger of suspicion at me since it was apparently known that I had been seen that day with matches in my hands. It didn't take long for the policeman to become quite sure I was guilty.

I remember my father taking me aside and saying, "I'm just going to ask the question once: did you have anything to do with the start of the fire?" My negative answer was all that he needed. He never asked a follow-up question. He never demanded any kind of proof. He never had to. My word was sufficient. He informed the police that I was not guilty, and they resumed their investigation. Later in the day, another boy confessed to the arson, and I learned the inestimable value of establishing my credibility.

I would like to suggest that my father was a foresightful man. He had known that there would come times when truth telling would be absolutely essential. In order to avoid impulsive reaction when a crisis arose, he had ground into me a regard for truth and the habit of facing it, no matter what the result. When the moment came in which truth was all-important, he could trust my word. That was my dad's day when foresight paid off. Mine too!

SHAPING THE WILL WITH WISDOM

CHARLES R. SWINDOLL

from *The Strong Family*

Keeping a proper balance in mind, there is yet another passage you should consider:

> "Do not hold back discipline from the child,
>   although you beat him with the rod, he will not die.
> You shall beat him with the rod, and deliver his soul from Sheol."
> (Proverbs 23:13–14 NASB)

It may surprise you to know that as I read that, I am relieved. If discipline is administered correctly, no parent should ever fear that death will result. When I hear of a child being abused so severely that he died, I know it was not biblical discipline that was used; it was an extreme, uncontrolled action of human insanity. God promises parents that death will not occur when they discipline His way. In fact, proper discipline will preserve your child from additional heartache! "Even though you smite him with the rod, you will deliver his soul from Sheol (or the place of death, the grave)." Discipline provides deliverance.

Rather than giving license to treat a child with brutality this guards us against it. This says, in effect, "Firmly punish when there has been willful defiance, and you have the assurance from God that your offspring will not die." Such discipline won't kill.

The Hebrew word *yah-saar*, translated "rod," troubled me when I first undertook this study years ago. I was bothered because it sounded harsh. And then I was relieved to know it is translated rod, because the Hebrew word means "club." (I suddenly became grateful my father did not know Hebrew in those days.) Don't overlook this: *yah-saar* calls for an implement when disciplining one's children. Perhaps we should think about that for a few moments.

During part of my growing-up years, my dad was a machinist. He had strong arms. When he spanked me, it was not with a switch or paddle, but with his hand. Perhaps that's the reason I lived much of my younger years in fear of my father—I identified my father with the pain of his punishment.

As we began to rear our children (and we so wanted to do it God's way), Cynthia and I decided we would always use a little paddle whenever we disciplined our children. The paddle we employed was connected to a little fly-back ball about the size of a ping-pong paddle. We'd remove the rubber tether and ball and then use only the paddle. We had several of them located in various spots in the house. For some strange reason they kept disappearing so we wound up having to hide them. That way they would always be in a safe place out of sight.

We followed a particular process, which I'll explain a little later. I am pleased to report that it worked: our children connected the pain to *the paddle* and not to us.

One time after I had spanked our younger daughter and we had worked through the whole thing, she was in her room getting ready to go to bed. Suddenly, she blurted out, "Daddy, come here!" I thought, *What in the world's wrong? What's she done . . . licked her night light?* I rushed into her room to find out the problem. Glaring at the paddle I had inadvertently left on her dresser, she cried; "Get that thing out of here!" Interestingly, she wanted me near, but not "that thing."

Maybe that's the reason God suggests the "rod" when disciplining. But you may still be unconvinced. You may still feel it unfair or somehow brutal to even strike your child or use any implement. You may fear that your youngster may question your love if you bring pain.

Stop and think for a moment of God's dealing with you and me. I remind you that God says He loves us, and whom He loves He *scourges* (Hebrews 12:6). Now *there* is a severe word! It could mean "takes the hide off." I know my heavenly Father loves me and cares for me. How do I know? When I act up, He gets me alone and skins my behind. Believe me, I never forget His thrashings. I need those times. If I were allowed to run roughshod over His prescribed will for me, and He let me get away with it, I would wonder if He really cared.

But to stay balanced, we must remember there should be verbal correction along with physical pain. It is necessary to add our words of reproof. Why would I suggest such a combination? Look at Proverbs 3:11–12:

> My son, do not reject the discipline of the Lord, or loathe His reproof, for whom the Lord loves He reproves, even as a father, the son in whom he delights.

What does all that mean? When you balance your discipline principles, you maintain not only a firm rod, but a faithful tongue. The two go together.

Periodically, I have heard people say, "There were times as a child when I got a spanking but didn't know why." That means the discipline lacked balance . . . a no-no! A child needs to be dealt with firmly when he has done wrong, but he always—yes, *always*—needs to know why. It is incorrect and unfair discipline when a child has no idea why he got a spanking.

It is extremely important for parents to remember that as the child grows older, there should be less and less physical punishment and more and more verbal correction. Once he reaches a level of maturity, there is no more paddling . . . only discussion. Your counsel changes from physical to verbal as your child matures. I should add this: There is no special age for all kids when this time comes. Some children have moved beyond the spanking phase when they reach the age of nine or ten. (I haven't met many, but there are some like that.) By the time the teen years arrive, you have gotten dangerously close to that fragile self-will where a paddle will do more harm than good. There are rare exceptions, of course.

Let's also understand that verbal correction is not a tongue-lashing. The Hebrew term means "to prove, to convince." We convince our child verbally that wrong is bad and cannot be tolerated. Remember, the statement in Proverbs concluded,

> For whom the Lord loves He reproves, even as a father, the son in whom he delights. (v. 12)

That's helpful. The word *delight* means "to approve of someone, to respect." It even means "to admire, to affirm." Does your child know you admire him or her? Your admiration helps them admire themselves. Affirmation works wonders!

BEULAH'S BULL CALF

CANDY ABBOTT

Mike, Jimmy, come quick!" I yelled through their bedroom door. "Dad says Beulah's having her calf right now!"

It was 1957, and I was ten. The smell of straw filled our nostrils as Mom and I scurried into our makeshift barn. The shed where we usually kept our tractor was now home to Beulah, the borrowed cow, and her newborn. Dad was busy wiping Beulah's back with a towel.

"Look over here," he said softly as my brothers, Jimmy and Mike, four and six years old, raced in to join us. On the other side of the cow was the ugliest, most wonderful hodgepodge of lanky legs, knobby knees, and slimy body I had ever seen. Beulah, the attentive mother, began licking her calf.

"Yuck!" Jimmy announced.

"It's not yucky," I said. "All babies are born with that stuff on them, and animals clean it off by licking. It's like giving them kisses."

"Is it a boy or a girl cow?" Mike asked.

"A boy cow isn't a cow," Dad explained. "It's a bull. And this is a bull calf."

"A bull calf!" Mike and Jimmy hopped around like kangaroos on a trampoline. "What are we gonna name him?"

"Calm down, boys," Dad said, "not so fast. I don't want you naming this calf *anything*."

"But, Dad, why not?" I asked on my brothers' behalf. "We always name our animals."

"Not this time, honey," he said. "I don't want you kids getting attached to this scrawny little fellow." He stopped rubbing Beulah, put the towel down, and walked around to where we were standing. When he knelt down to our level to look into our eyes, I knew it was serious.

Dad explained that he was boarding Beulah at no charge for a friend. In exchange, we got to keep the milk, butter, and cream that Mom pasteurized, churned, and whipped. The bargain included a promise that when the calf was born and grew to eighty pounds, Dad could take him to be butchered for veal for our family. We listened as though we understood what he was saying, mirroring his sad expression.

We were poor but didn't know it. Mom made me custom-fitted dresses, and I fancied myself the best-dressed girl in school. How was I to know the fabric often came from feed sacks? Dad might have been desperate for dollars, but he never seemed worried. He just did whatever he had to do to provide for us, like working three jobs.

As soon as the serious talk was over, we tiptoed over to the calf to *ooh* and *aah*, and secretly vowed to think up a good name for him.

Seven days a week, when the rooster crowed at sunrise, Dad would pull on his khaki pants and work boots, and then make his way to our backyard barn. The calf-with-no-name grew stronger each day. I prayed that he would stay small and never get to be eighty pounds. Every day, as Dad stirred up the mixture of ground corn and bran for Beulah, the bull calf would rub up against his thigh. In fact, every time he milked Beulah, the calf would nose around for attention.

One afternoon we overheard Dad telling Mom, "It's like that calf thinks I'm his mother." We noticed he would pat the calf on the head every now and then, but he still wouldn't let us name him.

"Hey, Mike; hey, Jimmy," I whispered a few minutes later, "I've got a good name for the bull calf. What do you think of 'Nosey'?"

From that moment on, Nosey became our secret pet.

Eventually, Dad taught me how to milk Beulah, and I took over the duty on Saturday mornings while Dad was plowing. Mike and Jimmy liked to stand around and watch me.

"Can I try it?" Mike asked.

"Sure," I said, feeling very grown up. "But you have to watch out for her hind legs so she doesn't kick you by mistake."

Jimmy entertained Nosey while Mike got into position, cautiously making his way around the towering cow. He perched proudly on the wooden three-legged stool under Beulah's fat tummy. Just as Dad had taught me, I leaned over and placed my hands around Mike's small fingers, demonstrating how to grip and pull and aim for the bucket.

"Ow!" Mike gasped as the warm milk sprayed his hand. "It's hot!"

"It's not hot," I said with a frown.

"Is too!" Mike insisted. It took us a while to realize he had expected it to come out of the cow cold, like it comes out of the refrigerator.

All too soon, the day came when the calf weighed eighty pounds. It was a Saturday morning, and Dad announced with a crack in his voice, "I guess I'll have to load him up."

"What do you mean, Daddy?"

"As much as I hate to do it, kids, I have to take the calf to the Town-send slaughterhouse."

"What's a slaughterhouse?"

"It's a place where they butcher livestock and wrap it to order. They have a meat locker and freezer, and do everything right there."

We still didn't understand what that had to do with Nosey.

As tenderly as he knew how, Dad said, "Remember when the calf was born, and I told you when he got big enough I'd have to have him butchered for veal? That means we have to kill the calf so we can live. We need meat for the winter."

"No!" I screamed and ran out of the room. "I'll never eat meat again!" I sobbed as I glanced over my shoulder with the meanest face I knew how to make.

I watched from my bedroom window as Dad walked resolutely but with slumped shoulders into the backyard and unlatched the barn door. I saw him wipe his cheek with the back of his hand. The calf innocently followed him outside and stood meekly beside our family car that doubled as a truck. It was a '48 Dodge Town & Country truck with a wooden station wagon body. I watched as Dad took out the backseat and folded down the middle one. He lifted Nosey's front legs, gave him a pat on the rear, and, like a child eager for a ride, the calf jumped over the tailgate. The grating clunk of metal as Dad slammed the tailgate echoed in my ears like a deathblow.

I was crying too hard to see him drive off. Mom came in to comfort me. She started to sit on the ruffled bedspread, but I waved her away. *How could she let him do this? Dear God,* I prayed, *don't let Nosey get butchered. Please do something to bring him back to us.*

Half an hour later, much sooner than expected, I heard the familiar sound of the station wagon engine and the crunch of tires in the driveway. And then I heard more noise than two young boys should be allowed to make, whooping and hollering as they slammed the screen door and raced into the kitchen.

"He's back!" Mike yelled. "Nosey's back!" Jimmy was grinning and jumping up and down. "Come and see!"

Sure enough, gangly legs and hooves were clambering their way over the station wagon tailgate, landing unsteadily and kicking up a small cloud of dust in the driveway. As Dad led Nosey by a short length of rope back to the barn to be reunited with his mother, the three of us hugged his neck and patted his silky ears. "What happened? What's he doing back?"

We couldn't tell if Dad was crying or laughing as he choked out an explanation. "The whole way into town, he kept rubbing his wet nose against my neck. I'd shoo him back, and the next thing I knew he'd be slobbering wet kisses all over my collar with that soft, fat tongue of his. I kept thinking, 'This is wrong. You can't do this, Jack. As much as you don't want to admit it, he's a family pet. You don't take pets to the butcher!' So I turned around, and here we are. What do you say we give this pet a name?"

"Dad," I giggled, looking at my brothers' excited faces, "we have a confession to make; we named him a long time ago. We call him Nosey!"

"Well, well," Dad said as he shook his head, "the perfect name. It was his wet nose on my neck that made me change my mind and bring him home."

My brothers and I learned a lot that day. We learned that daddies can change their minds. That daddies hear the heart-cry of their children. That daddies have feelings, too. That Abba, Daddy, our heavenly Father, answers prayer. Sometimes Daddy God says "no," like not keeping Nosey under eighty pounds. And sometimes he has a better plan.

Nosey grew up to be a fat, sassy bull that won several 4-H ribbons at the State Fair. Forty-three years later, I can still see Nosey's furry face in my mind's eye. And he's smiling.

A TIME TO UPROOT

CORRIE TEN BOOM

from *In My Father's House*

A time comes when all children, even a little Dutch girl with her jaw set and her black-stockinged legs rigid upon the staircase, must leave her father's house for a time. I was born with my feet slightly turned in, a defect which the doctor said would cure itself with time and growth.

"Don't worry," he told Mama and Papa, "when she is about sixteen, she will become vain enough to turn her toes the right way."

However, when I turned my toes in even more, and tightened my fingers in a knuckle-whitening grip on the railing, I meant business.

"I'm not going to school. I know how to read; I can learn arithmetic from Papa, and Casperina needs me at home."

There. *That* was settled.

"Of course you're not going to school alone, Corrie. I am going to walk with you."

Papa bent over me, his beard tickling the top of my head, and one by one loosened my fingers on the railing. With the release of each finger, I howled a bit louder. By the time Papa had my hand in his, he was almost dragging me down the street toward school. I thought my hand would break—just like Casperina's—and then it would be impossible for me to go to school.

It must have taken great dignity for Papa, with his immaculate suit and erect carriage, to struggle past the homes and shops of his friends with a red-faced child announcing her objections to the entire world.

I knew Father was not angry, but his will was law. I had to obey.

When we arrived at the school I saw a little boy being carried into Master Robyns's classroom in his father's arms. (At least I was walking!)

71

He was crying lustily, even louder than I was. He looked so ugly that I felt sorry for him. But what about me? I realized how I must look to others, and stopped abruptly.

Papa released my hand; my fingers weren't broken at all—only my heart was slightly injured. However, when Papa kissed me gently on the cheek, bringing the familiar fragrance of cigars and cologne, he assured me that when school was over, he would be waiting at home, and I knew I would find that blessed security I needed in the shelter of his arms.

God was teaching a little lesson in a small life, because sixty-seven years later, He reminded me of my fingers on the railing.

I was in a room of *Zonneduin*, a house in Holland, which some friends and I had established first for ex-prisoners who had been in concentration camps, and later for any person who needed nursing and rest. I had been traveling so much and was tired—tired of strange beds and different food—tired of dressing for breakfast—tired of new people, and new experiences. I liked this very luxurious house with its large rooms, and decided to stay, and enjoy the comfortable life in Holland, although I knew that God didn't agree with my decision.

Most of the furniture in the entire house was mine, but there was one room in particular that reminded me of the happy family life of my past. It was a room that held my treasures: photographs of those I loved, mementos of my family during the years before. Every picture was like the railing on the stairs. My hands grasped the past, and tried to hold on, but my heavenly Father's hands were stronger.

I left the house for a while for some speaking engagements, intending to return to my old room and settle in for good. However, when I came back to *Zonneduin* some weeks later, my pictures were down, and the strange belongings of someone else were on the bed.

My friends had not known of my personal decision to return to this room; my irregular life, my coming and going unexpectedly, was difficult for those who had to manage the big family of patients and staff in an orderly way.

But I decided to stay, and that was settled!

My heavenly Father spoke to me, "Only obey Me, Corrie. I'll hold your hand. It is My will that you leave your room. Later you will thank Me for this experience. You do not see it, but this is one of My great blessings for you."

Father's hand was firm, but I knew His love.

I packed up my suitcase again and left for the United States. How the Lord blessed my time there. Meetings began to grow in size, and when I saw people come from darkness into light, from bondage into liberation, I began to see the pattern. I could praise my Father that His hands were stronger than mine.

SECTION *Four*

The TEACHING
OF A FATHER

A LADDER TO THE CLOUDS

DR. BRUCE H. WILKINSON

from *The Prayer of Jabez*

One day when our kids were preschoolers, Darlene and I found ourselves with them at a large city park in southern California. It was the kind of park that makes a grown man wish he were a kid again. It had swings, monkey bars, and seesaws, but what was most enticing were the slides—not just one slide but three—from small, to medium, to enormous. David, who was five at the time, took off like a shot for the small slide.

"Why don't you go down with him?" Darlene suggested.

But I had another idea. "Let's wait and see what happens," I said. So we relaxed on a nearby bench and watched. David clambered happily to the top of the smallest slide. He waved over at us with a big smile, then whizzed down.

Without hesitation he moved over to the medium-sized slide. He had climbed halfway up the ladder when he turned and looked at me. I looked away. He pondered his options for a moment, then carefully backed down one step at a time.

"Honey, you ought to go help him out," my wife said.

"Not yet," I replied, hoping the twinkle in my eye would reassure her that I wasn't just being careless.

David spent a few minutes at the bottom of the middle slide watching other kids climb up, whiz down, and run around to do it again. Finally his little mind was made up. He could do it. He climbed up . . . and slid down. Three times, in fact, without even looking at us.

Then we watched him turn and head toward the highest slide. Now Darlene was getting anxious. "Bruce, I don't think he should do that by himself. Do you?"

"No," I replied as calmly as possible. "But I don't think he will. Let's see what he does."

When David reached the bottom of the giant slide, he turned and called out, "Daddy!" But I glanced away again, pretending I couldn't hear him.

He peered up the ladder. In his young imagination, it must have reached to the clouds. He watched a teenage boy go hurtling down the slide. Then, against all odds, he decided to try. Step-by-step, hand over hand, he inched up the ladder. He hadn't reached a third of the way when he froze. By this time, the teenager was coming up behind him and yelled at him to get going. But David couldn't. He couldn't go up or down. He had reached the point of certain failure.

I rushed over. "Are you okay, son?" I asked from the bottom of the ladder.

He looked down at me, shaken but clinging to that ladder with steely determination. And I could tell he had a question ready.

"Dad, will you come down the slide with me?" he asked. The teenager was losing patience, but I wasn't about to let the moment go.

"Why, son?" I asked, peering up into his little face.

"I can't do it without you, Dad," he said, trembling. "It's too big for me!"

I stretched as high as I could to reach him and lifted him into my arms. Then we climbed that long ladder up to the clouds together. At the top, I put my son between my legs and wrapped my arms around him. Then we went zipping down the slide together, laughing all the way.

HIS HAND, HIS SPIRIT

That is what your Father's hand is like. You tell Him, "Father, please do this in me because I can't do it alone! It's too big for me!" And you step out in faith to do and say things that could only come from His hand. Afterwards, your spirit is shouting, *God did that, nobody else! God carried me, gave me the words, gave me the power—and it is wonderful!*

THE PARADOX OF CHALLENGE AND ACCEPTANCE

WILL GLENNON

from *Fathering:*
Strengthening Connection With Your Children No Matter Where You Are

My sixteen-year-old daughter, who lives with her mother, called me the other day to tell me a dream she had. In her dream, she was in this very exotic village. In that village were many small shops with all manner of different goods for sale. She said that as she wandered through the village and looked at all the amazing things in the shops, she realized that she could have anything she wanted, because her father owned all the stores. It made her feel very happy, but she also said that the only thing she actually took was a set of beautiful luggage.

After telling me the dream, she asked me what I thought it meant. I told her I didn't think I should be the one to interpret this dream for her because I thought it was about me. She said she already knew that and persisted. I told her that the village was the world she was about to step into—a very beautiful, magical, and welcoming place. And that while she knew there were many presents she could take from me, the only one she needed was the luggage. As I finished, my voice was wavering with emotion and I told her that a father's job is to provide his children with good luggage.

We talked for a while longer, and I ended the call as I always have, saying, "I love you, sweetheart." She answered, "I love you too, Dad, and Dad, thanks for the luggage."

MY FATHER'S ARMS

H. MICHAEL BREWER

I've never seen God's arms, but I know what they are like because I remember my father's arms.

My father was a carpenter, his skin burned coffee brown to the edge of his T-shirt sleeves. My father had the skilled arms of a craftsman, and he moved with quiet confidence. From watching my father, I learned the value of a day's work, the beauty of the finishing touch, the joy of accomplishment.

I remember my father's arms, sheened with sweat, salted with sawdust, trembling with fatigue when long hours would scarcely keep food on the table. In later years my father's wrists swelled with arthritis, the legacy of swinging a hammer and pushing the heavy rotary saw, and the cost of providing for his family.

I remember my father's arms, muscled and powerful, strong enough to hoist a son into the air and settle him on sky-high shoulders. My father taught me to pass a football, cast a line, drive a nail. His arms were strong enough to be gentle, to hug the tears away, to hold the world at bay.

I remember my father's arms on the day my dog fell into a deep post-hole at a construction site. Lying on the ground, cheek pressed into the rough dirt, my father reached into the hole, strained until his fingertips snagged the dog's collar, and brought him back into the light. That day I believed my father could do anything and nothing was beyond his reach.

I remember my father's arms, scarred by flying nails, jagged wood, and rough work, the mementos of doing what must be done without complaints or excuses. My small fingers used to trace the calluses on his palms, and I learned that nothing worthwhile comes without effort. Even love is sometimes built on toil and blood.

I remember my father's arms side by side with my own. I held the plywood in place while he nailed. Staring straight at the work, he said, "I love you, and I'm proud of you." Our eyes didn't meet. There was no need. I squeezed his shoulder, and we both understood.

Much of what I know about God I learned from my father, from his arms, his deeds, his touch. Jesus' father was a carpenter too, and as a child Jesus must have learned about God from watching Joseph. No wonder many years later Jesus taught his disciples to think of God as a heavenly Father.

God loves us with a father's love and reaches out for us with a father's arms. God shapes us with the proud arms of a carpenter, a builder of worlds and ages. God guides us with the patient arms of a teacher, encouraging, coaxing, picking us up when we fall. God provides for us with faithful arms, putting food on the table and hope in the heart. God protects us with love-scarred arms, rescuing us from the pit, shielding us from the dark.

I've never seen God's arms, but I know what they are like because I remember my father's arms.

SEEKING AND FINDING

PHILIP GULLEY

from *Front Porch Tales*

My father is a leader of men. He exudes horse sense. When guidance is needed, my father's telephone rings. So when the Danville Mushroom Hunters Association was looking for leadership, they turned to my father.

"You must be our president, Norm," they said. "Everyone respects you. People turn to you for advice. Besides, you have a key to Lee Comer's cabin, and we were hoping we could go there this weekend."

The nomination was made. The vote taken. Five to zero, a veritable landslide.

They left for the cabin on a Friday night, stopping on the way to purchase a gallon of wine in obedience to Saint Paul's advice to young Timothy. Ordinarily, these are not religious men, except when it comes to 1 Timothy 5:23; then they are fundamentalists to the core.

Dad woke them up at 4:30 the next morning. Any mushroom hunter worth his salt knows that alone of all the mushroom family, the morel is at its finest in the early morning hours. Once the sun rises, the morel loses its appeal. It's a nocturnal mushroom. When the sun hits a morel, it's done for, but if you pick it while it's still wet with morning dew and get it into briny water within an hour or so, you'll enjoy an unrivaled delicacy. You have to plan accordingly.

The first mistake many mushroom hunters make is their failure to organize. Fortunately, Dad came prepared.

"To begin with, we need a vision statement," he said. "Every organization worth its salt has one. I would like to suggest 'Semper Fidelus' or 'Always Faithful.' " Dad watched a lot of Marine movies. They voted. It was unanimous; not a person disagreed. Mostly because their heads hurt

81

too much from heeding Saint Paul the night before.

After breakfast, they went to the woods. The morel mushroom is one of nature's more elusive quarries. Buckskin-clad men at one with nature have been reduced to tears in their search for this Holy Grail of the mushroom family. Children, however, have been known to stumble upon entire acres of this delicacy only to return as adults and not find even the smallest spore of a morel. The memory of it haunts them in their sleep.

The first day's search proved fruitless, as did the next day's. They went home more or less morel-less. Dad, being a leader of men, called an emergency meeting of the D.M.H.A. that week. He sat at the head of the table pondering their failure. One of the members ventured an idea: "Maybe next time we should go when the snow is off the ground."

"Don't bother me," Dad replied. "I'm thinking, and what I'm thinking is that we need a new vision statement. You can do just about anything with a good vision statement. How about 'Semper Investigare, Nunquam Invenire'?" Dad thought he knew Latin from watching movies about Latin America.

"Sounds good, Norm," they said. "What's it mean?"

"It's Latin," he said. "It means 'Always Searching, Never Finding.'"

That being something they could live up to, the vote was unanimous.

In the Bible it talks about knocking and the door will be opened. I've met some folks for whom that is true. Folks who stumble upon the holy like children upon morels. But for every one of those happy finders, I've met a weary knocker. Lifelong seekers whose knuckles are bloody-raw in their quest for the divine.

Sometimes they come by to talk. They flop down in a rocker and ask why God seems silent. I never know what to tell them, other than to keep on looking, that God works at God's pace. I point out that sometimes good things come easy, but not usually. So it's a matter of persevering, of not discouraging, of organizing your life to increase your chances of finding.

I didn't learn that from the Bible. I learned it from my dad, while traipsing through light-dappled woods in search of the Holy Grail.

WATER HEATER
MOMENTS

CLARK COTHERN

from *Detours*

S *plash*

"Oh, my goodness."

My dad took one more step inside the front door. Hearing another splash, he said again, only slower, and with even more tension in his voice, "Ohhh, my gooooodness."

Following him into the living room of our Phoenix house, our feet felt the cause of his broken-record behavior.

First my mother, then my sister, then me. We each stepped in, and as though reading from the same cue card, we each said, in succession, "Oh—my—goodness."

It felt as if we were back in Oak Creek Canyon. *In* the creek.

Dad flipped the light switch and suddenly, my sleepy eyes popped wide open. The warm, comfortable thoughts of turning in for the night vanished like a good dream when the alarm clock goes off.

A half-inch of water stood where there used to be a floor.

In the living room. In the hall. Everywhere.

If we had lived in Alaska, we could have turned the house into a hockey rink. But this was Phoenix. A little too warm for hockey.

We had just driven an hour from Arlington. It had been a typical marathon Sunday: Up early, drive to church, set up, light the gas heaters, help with Sunday school, over to a member's house for lunch, visiting folks all over the countryside all afternoon, back to church for the evening service. Then, on our way home, we stopped at the Mattinglys' who owned the Hassyampa convenience market. They had fed us dinner, which consisted of ham-and-cheese refrigerated sandwiches in cellophane wrappers, warmed in the microwave.

It was nearly eleven and all of us were whipped.

All I wanted to do was crawl into bed. In fact, if I'd been smaller, I probably would have asked for someone to carry me there. But this unusual turn of events was about to rain on our parade—and on our bedtime. To be accurate, it even soaked the dust ruffles on our beds.

We had just been detoured from a typical Sunday night road, which normally dead-ends into a good night's sleep, down Soggy Street into a waterlogged house.

It took a minute for Dad to figure out where the water was coming from. He stood there, scratching his head, and repeating the phrase, "Oh, my goodness," and then suddenly he put his finger up to his lips and said, "Shh. Listen."

We all stood there feeling the water soak into our socks, like a family of bird dogs trying to catch the scent of a pheasant. Noses in the air, heads swiveling back and forth, as though we would hear better at different angles.

Then we heard it. The sound of water running.

It sounded as if someone had brought in the garden hose and turned it on ever so slightly. It just ran, like a steady small stream, into the ocean of floor.

Like a super sleuth with supersonic hearing, Dad followed the sound through the living room and into the hall, where he stopped. We all followed, tiptoeing our way across the living room, where a couple of magazines floated by the coffee table. Halfway down the hall, Dad held up his hand like a platoon leader stopping his men on the trail behind him. I paused with one foot out of the water, frozen like a flamingo. Then he turned his head toward the hall closet.

"There!" he shouted triumphantly. And he whipped open the door.

I don't know what he expected to find there. Perhaps an evil neighbor, sabotaging our house by holding the garden hose in the hall closet?

There was no neighbor. But we did see the source of our woes. A round, curved disk floated like a little steel ship on the water inside the closet. It was about as big around as one of those snow disks you use to careen down a wintry slope.

The bottom of our water heater.

Dad explained, "It looks like it simply rusted out. It got so corroded that the whole seam just let loose."

I said, "Too bad it hasn't learned how to hold its water."

Smart-mouth kid. Everyone groaned.

Dad continued, "The pipe that refills the tank when it goes down hasn't gotten the message that there is no bottom in the heater, so it's just doing its job like it's supposed to."

Everyone looked at me, waiting for another wisecrack.

I just looked surprised and said, "What? I'm just listening."

"Lucky for us the house isn't watertight," Dad added.

"Why's that?" we all asked at the same time.

"Well, the pipe would have continued to fill up what it thought was the tank until the water level was about five feet high, when a float would have finally stopped it."

"That would have been awesome," I said.

They all looked at me again.

"Well. It would have."

"Lucky for us," Dad summed up, "our back door doesn't seal very well at the threshold, so I'll bet most of the excess water is seeping out the back door, onto the patio, and out into the backyard."

"Guess we won't have to use the sprinkler for a few days, huh?" I said.

Though very tired, and in a vulnerable state of mind, Dad surprised us all. He began barking orders like a captain directing his crew. His brisk good humor in that situation was infectious.

"You, first mate," he said, pointing at me, "grab a towel from the bathroom and start swabbing the deck."

"Aye, aye, Cap'n. But where's the deck?"

"Uh, the bathroom," he said. "Start sopping up the water in the bathroom and wring out the towel into the toilet, because that will carry the water down below the floor level."

I saluted and stumped off, peg-leg style, toward the bathroom.

"You, helmsman," he said, pointing to my sister, "grab the keys to the toolshed. I'll head to the backyard to retrieve the tools necessary to fix the pipe."

And to my mother he said (in a much less demanding tone), "Dear, would you mind getting the flashlight so I can see to turn off the water?"

I guess he had either run out of nautical terms or he was being extra polite with Mom. He must have known that it's always better to ask nicely when it comes to your wife.

Considering the lateness of the hour and the tiredness of all the crew, it could have been a much stickier, much more unhappy situation than it really was. We could have all been totally disgusted with the whole thing, sniping at each other, and sloshing around in our soaking-wet attitudes for days.

But thanks to my Dad's attitude toward it all, the detour turned into a family adventure. None of us will ever forget it.

There we were, on our soaking-wet knees, wringing out bath towels into the toilets in both bathrooms, singing, in harmony, "There shall be showers of blessing."

Dad did the right thing, and it amazes me as I look back on that situation. He laughed off what couldn't be changed and set us all to work . . . together.

Our little adventure up Water Heater Creek revealed to me that leaks in life just happen.

Leaky water heaters happen.

Leaky radiator hoses happen.

Leaky diapers happen (sometimes on your good clothes right before you leave for a special evening).

And often, it's nobody's fault.

Dad's water heater didn't cook up a scheme to see how far over the emotional edge it could push my dad after a long, hard day. It didn't hide in the hall closet, whispering to its cousin, the air conditioner, "Psst. Hey, A.C. Listen up. It's all set. It's goin' down tonight. At precisely 8:34. That's when I'm going to drop the bottom out of my tank and flood the joint. It's the perfect time, because the owners will be gone all day. Boy, will they get what's coming to them when *they* get home."

Sometimes the way we react to life's little leaks (and some of the big ones), you'd think inanimate objects had minds of their own. But they don't.

My dad recognized that what Chuck Swindoll says is true: "Life is 10 percent what happens to you and 90 percent how you respond to it."

He's as right as rain.

My rule of thumb, after our anchor-dropping, bilge-pumping evening, is this: *If the detour doesn't involve the loss of life or limb, and if it's only water you hear dripping—not blood—then laugh it off.*

Change what's changeable, and laugh off the rest. Hey, it worked for Dad, and it rubbed off on the rest of us that night.

MY FATHER'S TOOLS

VALERIE KELLY

I was elated, joyous, jubilated!

I was freeeee!

I had just experienced all the pomp and circumstance that befalls a college graduate, and I was heady about all the possibilities that lay before me. I was leaving the Midwest for Fort Lauderdale, Florida, in search of a job and needed reliable transportation to get me there. I asked my father to help me choose an appropriate vehicle for my adventure, which is how I found out that my dear old dad, who is very reliable in most situations, was not in this one.

Since he was not of a mechanical nature—nor I, being the daughter he raised—both of us floundered. Do you buy one that looks appealing on the outside and hope the engine has that same quality? Do you look at the miles and the price comparatively? Is there a universal formula for used car buying that no one told us about?

After much chin stroking, we selected a sky blue, eight-year-old Dodge Arrow with two bright white racing stripes painted on the sides. It had a good paint job and four new tires. We took it for a road test. As we hit the interstate, the engine became very loud, but for some crazy reason, he thought this meant it was working. Despite the fact that Dad was as clueless as I, I was so happy to be a car owner and one step closer to Florida that I didn't care how questionable this little gem may have been.

As soon as we parked it in the driveway, I began cramming it with packed boxes of summer wear and swim suits, a treasured photo album, clock radio, toiletries, and a good interviewing business suit for landing a job. All the essentials I needed to embark on my southern expedition.

As my swollen vehicle nestled a little lower to the ground, I finished my packing. I purposely saved the front seat floor space for the fundamental basics—chips, diet soda, Rand McNally Atlas, tote bag, and a calling card to check in with Mom. But someone had taken the liberty of placing a box of tools there.

It wasn't just a standard cardboard box, or even a shoebox, but a flimsy, crumpled-corner shirt box (sans the crumpled cover) that a week earlier had been a casing for a Christmas present. I knew it was my father who had bequeathed this intriguing array of gadgets to me.

The tools inside the poor container were aged and worn. Scars and notches on the wooden handles from past use were apparent. *Okay, Dad,* I thought sarcastically to myself, *exactly what am I supposed to do with these tools?* He left no instructions for them, and to be honest, I'm sure he wouldn't have known what to do with them or how to use them anyway. For heaven's sake, he didn't even put them in a toolbox, but in an old, worn-out, Christmas box! Nor could I imagine what I needed these tools for or what I would do with them.

My father came up behind me as I studied this mysterious addition. I could tell by the way he stood beside me with his head cocked forward to observe, humming to himself as he does absentmindedly, that he had picked the tools judiciously and purposely. The box held two hammers (a big, bulky one with a long rubber-gripped handle and a medium-sized one that had three small flat-head screwdrivers nestled in the handle), several wrenches of various sizes, a needle-nosed pliers, a Phillips-head screwdriver, floral wire, a pack of nails of varying lengths, a sharp cutting knife, and a few other choice instruments.

As I watched him scrutinize my inheritance, I realized this gift was an extension of my father's love for me. These tools were his father's tools. My grandfather repaired Singer sewing machines during the '30s and '40s. His career was beginning to soar after World War II ended and women were anxious to make homes attractive for their returning veterans. Unfortunately, bone cancer abruptly stopped his father and his career. My father lost his father when he was seventeen—on the day of his high school graduation. In those days, children were not allowed to visit in hospitals. Three days after his father was admitted to the hospital, his mother returned to tell my dad and his two younger brothers that their father had died. Dad didn't even get a chance to say good-bye.

My father is not always an affectionate man. I think he frequently doesn't know what to do or what to say. However, I understood the gesture he bestowed upon me on that winter day. He was keeping me safe, preparing me for the next phase of life, and saying good-bye the best way he knew how.

I can close my eyes and still see that crumpled shirt box filled with my father's tools. And much to my surprise and delight, those carefully chosen tools did prove useful in the most mundane, but efficient, ways. I used them to hang up pictures on the walls, to cut floral wire for a holiday decoration, and to repair a piece of second-hand furniture. It seems apparent now that though I didn't know the possibilities of those tools, my father did. And, thanks to him, they were there when I needed them.

Twenty years have passed since that memory, and I realize that not only did my earthly father provide me with tools to make my life easier but my heavenly Father did also. He equipped me with spiritual tools: a deep faith that God's will *will* be done, the power of prayer, and the assurance that I am never alone. He equipped me with earthly tools as well: a devoted and loving husband, wonderful friends, and parents who have nourished my relationship with God.

It is all of these tools that I have used to cope with life's sorrows and to celebrate life's joys. I have come to realize that our Father gives us tools every day. At the time, we may not understand how to use them or what to use them for. Yet if we are quiet and listen to the voice of the Father, we will know that He has given us the necessary tools to complete our journey here on earth.

SECTION Five

The FORGIVENESS OF A FATHER

A HOME, A GIFT

MOTHER TERESA

from *In the Heart of the World: Thoughts, Stories, and Prayers*

Some young people who ran away from home have gotten sick with AIDS. We have opened a home in New York for AIDS patients, who find themselves among the most unwanted people of today.

What a tremendous change has been brought about in their lives just because of a few sisters who take care of them, and have made a home for them!

A home of love!

A gift of love!

A place, perhaps the only place, where they feel loved, where they are somebody to someone. This has changed their lives in such a way that they die a most beautiful death. Not one of them has yet died in distress.

The other day, a sister called to tell me that one of the young men was dying. But, strange to say, he couldn't die. He was struggling with death.

So she asked him, "What is it? What is wrong?"

And he said, "Sister, I cannot die until I ask my father to forgive me."

So the sister found out where the father was, and she called him. And something extraordinary happened, like a living page from the Gospel: The father came and embraced his son and cried, "My son! My beloved son!"

And the son begged the father, "Forgive me!"

Two hours later the young man died.

THE FATHER'S LOVE

DAN THIESSEN

A young boy and his sister were digging tunnels one day. They were in a place they were not supposed to be, doing what they were told not to do. Bradley was digging, while his younger sister Chrissy complained from above.

"Daddy's going to be so mad at you, Bradley Jackson. You're not supposed to be digging tunnels. Daddy said."

Bradley kept digging, ignoring his younger sister like he usually did when he was busy. Then Chrissy got angry that she was being ignored. She jumped up and down just above where Bradley was digging. The more Bradley ignored her, the more Chrissy raised her voice to a fever pitch.

"Daddy's going to be so mad at you!" Her jumping up and down found a rhythm that inspired her to scold her brother like a nursery rhyme.

"Daddy's gonna be mad! Daddy's gonna be mad! When he comes, ta da dum dee dum, Daddy's gonna be mad!"

She sang over and over as she jumped up and down. Bradley was now directly beneath her, but she had closed her eyes while singing at the top of her voice and hadn't noticed.

Then the ground gave way, trapping the boy below. As the earth fell in, one of his hands instinctively covered his mouth while the other reached for the surface. Immobilized by a mound of dirt with only a hand exposed, the boy feared for his life. Amazingly, there was an air pocket, but how long would the air last?

He tried to move his exposed hand, finger by finger, trying to signal Chrissy, trying to give her some sign of life. But when he couldn't hear her voice or feel her footsteps on the ground above him, he hoped Chrissy had run to get help.

So this is what it's like to die. I don't want to die. I'm afraid to die. But what if I live? What if Dad comes and finds me here? What if he finds that I've been playing where he told me not to play? I've disappointed him again. He's going to be angry. He's going to be so angry.

Bradley waited impatiently in the dark.

At the house, Chrissy was nearly out of breath when she reached her father, who was working in the farm implement shed.

"Daddy, Daddy, don't be mad. Please, don't be mad."

"What is it, Chrissy? What's the matter?" Joe Jackson said as he laid aside his tools and lowered himself to Chrissy's level.

"Bradley, he, he—" Chrissy was out of breath.

"Take me to him." Joe picked up Chrissy and ran in the direction she was pointing.

The first thing the father did was to grasp Bradley's hand. Bradley felt the squeeze and weakly tried to squeeze back.

Joe began digging with one hand while continuing to comfort with the other. After he freed Bradley, he carried him back to the house. Not a word was said. Laying his son down on his bed and brushing the dirt from his face, his eyes began to moisten as he turned away in embarrassment.

"I thought I was going to die, Dad. Then I thought how mad you were going to be at me."

Bradley's words hurt Joe deep inside. Joe remained with his head turned away from his son. Bradley reached for his hand.

"But when you grabbed my hand, Dad, I knew everything was going to be all right. Thanks, Dad."

Overcome with emotion, Joe leaned over and hugged Bradley. His tears flowed unabashed. Gently wiping the dirt and tears from Bradley's face, Joe just stared into his son's eyes. He stared long enough to see himself.

Not long ago, when life seemed dark and caving in around him, he felt the hand of his heavenly Father grasp his, assuring him things would be all right. It was difficult at that time for Joe to believe God would love him that much.

Today he understood that love.

"Where can I go from your Spirit? Where can I flee from your presence? If I go up to the heavens, you are there; if I make my bed in the depths, you are there. If I rise on the wings of the dawn, if I settle on the far side of the sea, even there your hand will guide me, your right hand will hold me fast." (Psalm 139:7–10)

AT THE FATHER'S TABLE

BOB HOSTETLER

Once upon a time, there was a young man named Seth who had a brilliant future, a best friend . . . and a nice, fast car.*

One winter evening Seth picked up his friend Jason in his car. He and Jason both played in their high school concert band; Seth was a clarinetist and Jason played the trumpet. They were dressed in white shirts and ties for a holiday concert.

Jason slid into the front seat of Seth's car.

"You ready for this?" Seth asked as he put the car into gear and pulled out from in front of Jason's house.

"Yeah," Jason answered easily. "I finally got that lick down."

"The one in *Carol of the Bells?*"

Jason nodded.

The two close friends bantered with each other as Jason navigated the short drive to the high school. They would be warming up in the band room in just a few minutes.

As they approached a sharp bend in the road, something happened. It may have been the headlights of the car that had passed them just before they reached the curve. It may have been a slick spot on the pavement. It may have been a momentary lapse of judgment. It may have been the speed of the car, nothing more.

Seth was going a little too fast as he entered the curve. In an instant of time that would later be forgotten, he lost control of the car. The vehicle veered wide, off the pavement, and smashed into a tree.

Within a few seconds after the accident, one of the boy's teachers, who

---

*A true story

had been driving to the same concert, arrived at the scene. Seth was already out of the car, stumbling, bloodied, crying Jason's name.

The teacher used both hands to wrench Jason's door open and saw immediately that the boy was hurt badly. He eased the teenager from the car and cradled his head in his arms. Jason's labored breathing slowed, then stopped, and the teacher's efforts to revive him failed. When the emergency squad arrived at the scene, Jason was dead.

Hundreds of Jason and Seth's classmates attended the funeral a few days later. Seth, who had been released from the hospital only that morning, sobbed through the ceremony. As he left the funeral, he reached the double doors of the sanctuary . . . just as Jason's grieving mother and father entered the doorway from the other side.

Seth saw his friend's parents, and fell into the arms of Jason's father, a Christian minister. The man, his face twisted by his own grief, hugged the boy.

"I'm so sorry," Seth cried in anguish. "I killed your son. I killed your only son."

The crowd surrounding the pair averted their eyes from the scene. The father hushed Seth's cries as he hugged him. "I forgive you, Seth," he said. "I want you to forgive yourself."

The father not only spoke forgiveness to the boy but he also demonstrated it. In the months and years that followed, Jason's father regularly invited Seth to dinner with him and his wife. Over time, the father's forgiveness helped Seth to forgive himself, and some things in his life returned to normal. But one thing would forever be different.

Seth came to love Jason's parents as if they were his own. And they loved him. But Seth never took a bite at their table, never sipped a drink, without remembering his friend, without being awed at the father's grace and forgiveness.

Seth's story parallels another, and it's mine . . . and yours.
You see, many years ago, my sins killed the Father's only Son. It was

for my negligence, my rebellion, my failings that he died.

And yet in spite of that, the Father not only forgives me but he also demonstrates his love and forgiveness by inviting me to his table and by allowing me to partake of a meal, to commune with him.

And though my life may look more or less the same in many ways, one thing will be forever different. I will never take a piece of bread or drink a drop of wine at the Lord's table without remembering my Friend, and without being awed at the Father's grace and forgiveness that would allow me to come to his table.

RESTORATION

ELIZABETH MARVIN

A series of howling shrieks from our two-year-old daughter shattered the evening's peace and quiet. Her brother's taunting and teasing had been escalating over the past few days. Patience had never been her strength, and he had pushed her to the breaking point. My husband put a sudden end to the mischief with a stern command: "Young man, go to your room!"

Our son sniffled once or twice, and his large brown eyes, so like his father's, filled up with tears. But he manfully turned and headed for the steps. A few seconds later, his door closed.

My husband calmly continued reading the newspaper, while my heart ached for the little one upstairs. He had never been punished like this in all of his four years, but I supposed it was time. I wondered what he was feeling. It wasn't difficult for me to imagine, since I'd occupied a similar room so many times myself during my own childhood.

After ten minutes my husband put down his paper and stood up. "Where are you going?" I asked, surprised.

"Upstairs to the guilty party," he answered with a smile. "He's been there long enough. It's time for his father to restore him."

It wasn't until my husband left that his last words really sank in. And then I found to my surprise that I was weeping.

In my mind I was a child again, banished to solitary confinement while the room darkened around me with the encroaching dusk. There I was, once more out of favor with my small universe. I was crushed by the familiar burden of guilt and shame. I knew that if I crept out, begging, I would finally be readmitted into the light of my parents' presence. But something inside me always rebelled. I chose instead to maintain my stubborn separation.

In the end I pretended, as we all did, that the terrible rupture had never occurred. Like a broken teacup, our family fitted itself back together time and time again, but we were never permanently glued. We balanced on the shelf-edge of conditional love.

I had never realized there could be any other ending. I wondered, *What if the door I could never bring myself to open had been opened for me? What if, into that widening rectangle of light, my own father had come, with a message of love and restoration?*

I sobbed, rocked by waves of gratitude and grief. The overwhelming yearning that had dogged my heart since childhood was finally defined. I saw myself—God's shamed and lonely child—now standing in the light of a wide open door. Finally, in the healing warmth that radiated from the cross, I heard God's voice echo in the words of my husband.

"It's been long enough. It's time for the Father to restore you."

My husband returned with our son in his arms, and they were laughing.

"I'M SORRY!"

ROBERT H. SCHULLER

from *The Be (Happy) Attitudes*

When you learn to make this confession, you'll find happiness, because you will discover the miracle-working power to be an honest person. You and I are free when we admit we've been wrong. Instead of an ego trip, we are on an integrity trip—the road to real happiness. For the integrity trip really feeds our self-esteem. We can be proud of ourselves for being open and honest and humble! By contrast, the ego trip is a constant threat and finally fatal to genuine self-respect!

On the integrity trip we're no longer slaves to perfectionism. So we aren't embarrassed when people catch us making mistakes. When we have done something wrong, we need only say, "I'm sorry." To the ones we've hurt we can say, "I'm a human being. The Lord has forgiven me. I've forgiven myself; I hope you will too."

I will never forget the morning I asked my oldest daughter, Sheila, to do the breakfast dishes before school. Not realizing that she was already running late and facing too many tardy notices, I was stunned by her reaction. She burst into profuse tears.

Again, misinterpreting the motive behind the outburst, assuming that she was merely trying to get out of an unpleasant chore, I demanded that she dry her eyes and get to work—*immediately.*

She reluctantly obeyed me, but I could hear her anger in the careless clanking of the dishes in the sink. On the way to school, she turned her back to me and stared sullenly out the window.

Usually, I took positive advantage of the uninterrupted time that I was able to spend with my children while driving them to school by teaching them poetry or Bible verses or just sharing together.

On that morning, however, there were no poems, no verses, no songs—only deathly, stubborn silence. I dropped Sheila off, mumbled a good-bye, and left for my office. I tried to work, but I couldn't concentrate. All I could see was the scared, tear-stained face of my daughter as she hesitantly climbed out of the car to face her teacher and classmates.

I had begun to realize that my timing had been way off. I had no right to demand that she do the dishes without giving her some forewarning, some planning time. I realized that I had been wrong to upset her so close to the time when she was going to be facing peers, a time when she needed support.

The more I thought about it, the more remorseful I became. Finally, I decided that I had to do something. I had to say I was sorry, and my apology could not wait until suppertime. So, I called the school and I asked the counselor for permission to take her to lunch.

I shall never forget the look of surprise on her face when she saw me waiting for her in the office. I said, "Sheila, I've gotten permission to take you to lunch. They said that you could have an hour off. Let's go."

I led her by the arm down the empty school corridor. As soon as the heavy doors slammed behind us, I turned to my daughter and I said, "Sheila, I'm sorry. I'm so very sorry! It's not that I shouldn't have asked you to help out at home, but I had no right to insist on it this morning without any previous warning. I upset you at a time when you most needed my love and support—just before you went to school. And I let you go without saying 'I love you.' I was wrong. Please forgive me."

Sheila put her arms around my neck and hugged me and said, "Oh, Dad, of course I forgive you. I love you, too."

Oh, the power of those restorative words, "I'm sorry!" They heal relationships—between ourselves and our friends and loved ones, and between ourselves and our Lord.

ABBA, DADDY

LILLY GREEN

A light dusting of snow drifted in through the wooden boards that formed the small back porch of our woodshed. I huddled on the hard ground underneath the porch, cold and out of sight, punishing myself.

Down at the corner store next to the main highway, I had curiously peeked into the centerfold of one of their "dirty" magazines. Guilt attached itself to my young, tender conscience like a leech in lake water. Shivering, afraid to go into the house, I watched the winter sun fall silently behind the ragged tree-lined horizon.

In spite of my warm winter clothing, damp cold and stiffness invaded my tight, lonely space. No one would find me out here behind the shed, and I guess I really did want to be found, so I scrambled over the wood slabs to the front entrance of the woodshed. Daddy would be coming along soon to do chores. I hid in the darkness and waited. As he walked by, heading toward the barn, I gave a little artificial whimper to signal my presence. Daddy stopped and peeked around the doorjamb.

"What are you doing all alone out here in the cold?" he asked.

I was more than ready to confess. "Well, I . . . I mean, I looked at dirty pictures at the store. I didn't mean to, and I thought you and Mom would be mad, and so I. . . ." The words came in frosted puffs while tears flowed down my rosy cheeks.

"Honey, there's no need to hide. No sin's too big for God to forgive. Just ask Him now, and it's done. Just like that!"

I mumbled a prayer as Daddy engulfed me in his strong arms and bulky winter coat. The burden flew from my shoulders. Together we walked to the barn to do the chores. He milked the cows, while I carried the milk to the cooler.

Several years later another experience demonstrated to me my father's fierce, unconditional love.

While attending summer school at a strict Christian college, I found myself alone and lonely on a Fourth of July weekend. Most students had returned home for parties and fireworks, and only a few of us remained at the school. Home was too far away to swing by for a weekend foray.

I ran into two girls who told me spooky stories of a car they'd sighted circling the dorms. They had worked themselves up into a frenzy and were afraid to be alone, so I decided to be hospitable. I invited them to spend the night with me in my tiny apartment. A couple of miles off campus, down a country road, it was situated in an isolated row of apartments. That invitation was my first mistake.

My second mistake was to allow another acquaintance to invite himself over for ice cream and a TV movie. The six-pack was his idea.

Though I didn't drink, he imbibed a fair amount, enough to be goofy and uninhibited. His drinking, which was not exactly college policy, caused my "friends" some anxiety. He broke into the bedroom where they lay gabbing in pajamas and rollers. Apparently, he made rather suggestive comments to my two paranoid houseguests, which only increased their fears. They locked him out, and we proceeded to watch our movie. Unbeknownst to us, the girls, "fearing for their lives," cut the screen in my back bedroom window and escaped on foot into the black night and back to the dorms.

The story they told school officials must have been a very dramatic one, for I was marshaled in before the dean of students to give an account. After a lengthy session on the consequences of disobeying school rules, I was disciplined by being placed on social probation and given the choice to inform my parents myself or have the school call. I called.

I heard the phone ringing—a long and a short on our party line. My throat tightened as I rehearsed my words and waited for someone to pick up. Finally Daddy answered the call from this tearful collegian five hundred long miles away.

"Daddy, it's me. I'm in trouble." I spoke softly into the receiver, as my tears fell.

"Lillian, is that you? What in the world is the matter; are you hurt, or. . . ?"

"No, no . . . I'm okay; it's just that . . . well, I did something stupid, and the school threatened to kick me out, but I didn't do anything myself, really . . . I mean, I did, but I. . . ." With stops and starts I explained the hurtful situation, not diminishing my error and lack of judgment. Then I paused, waiting for his response.

"Oh, honey, I'm so sorry you're going through all of this. You know your mom and I trust you and love you." I heard the tears in his voice. "I wish I could be there right now to hold you. If it wasn't so far, I'd be down there tonight. You know that, don't you?"

"Yes, Daddy, I know." I swallowed over the lump in my throat. "I love you, Daddy."

Absolution had come quickly, just as it had on that cold winter's night years before.

My dad may never completely understand what his affirmation did for me. In that tender moment, the burden lifted. I was loved—accepted, no matter what.

He could have given me the speech about guilt by association, or about the evils of alcohol, or any number of speeches. I know how they go, because as a parent myself now, I've given a few to my own boys. But that wasn't Daddy's way. He knew I had punished myself enough. I was already aware of the unwise choices I'd made. He knew I needed comfort, not criticism.

At other times in my life when I have felt alone, ill at ease, trying to find my way in this crazy world, my father has been there with his unconditional love—arms outstretched. When I have been deeply hurt by those I trusted or filled with doubt through a death or other loss, he has made it easy to believe in a loving heavenly Father—a Father who invites us to call him Abba, Daddy.

SECTION Six

The PERSPECTIVE OF A FATHER

SEEING WHAT EYES CAN'T

MAX LUCADO

from *When God Whispers Your Name*

I stand six steps from the bed's edge. My arms extended. Hands open. On the bed Sara—all four years of her—crouches, posed like a playful kitten. She's going to jump. But she's not ready. I'm too close.

"Back more, Daddy," she stands and dares.

I dramatically comply, confessing admiration for her courage. After two giant steps I stop. "More?" I ask.

"Yes!" Sara squeals, hopping on the bed.

With each step she laughs and claps and motions for more. When I'm on the other side of the canyon, when I'm beyond the reach of mortal man, when I am but a tiny figure on the horizon, she stops me. "There, stop there."

"Are you sure?"

"I'm sure," she shouts. I extend my arms. Once again she crouches, then springs. Superman without a cape. Skydiver without a chute. Only her heart flies higher than her body. In that airborne instant her only hope is her father. If he proves weak, she'll fall. If he proves cruel, she'll crash. If he proves forgetful, she'll tumble to the hard floor.

But such fear she does not know, for her father she does. She trusts him. Four years under the same roof have convinced her he is reliable. He is not superhuman, but he is strong. He is not holy, but he is good. He's not brilliant, but he doesn't have to remember to catch his child when she jumps.

And so she flies.

And so she soars.

And so he catches her and the two rejoice at the wedding of her trust and his faithfulness.

I stand a few feet from another bed. This time no one laughs. The room is solemn. A machine pumps air into a tired body. A monitor metronomes the beats of a weary heart. The woman on the bed is no child. She was, once. Decades back. She was. But not now.

Like Sara, she must trust. Only days out of the operating room, she's just been told she'll have to return. Her frail hand squeezes mine. Her eyes mist with fear.

Unlike Sara, she sees no father. But the Father sees her. Trust him, I say to us both. Trust the voice that whispers your name. Trust the hands to catch.

I sit across the table from a good man. Good and afraid. His fear is honest. Stocks are down. Inflation is up. He has payroll to meet and bills to pay. He hasn't squandered or gambled or played. He has worked hard and prayed often, but now he's afraid. Beneath the flannel suit lies a timid heart.

He stirs his coffee and stares at me with the eyes of Wile E. Coyote who just realized he's run beyond the edge of a cliff. He's about to fall and fall fast. He's Peter on the water, seeing the storm and not the face. He's Peter in the waves, hearing the wind and not the voice.

Trust, I urge. But the word thuds. He's unaccustomed to such strangeness. He's a man of reason. Even when the kite flies beyond the clouds he still holds the string. But now the string has slipped. And the sky is silent.

I stand a few feet from a mirror and see the face of a man who failed . . . who failed his Maker. Again. I promised I wouldn't, but I did. I was quiet when I should have been bold. I took a seat when I should have taken a stand.

If this were the first time, it would be different. But it isn't. How many times can one fall and expect to be caught?

Trust. Why is it easy to tell others and so hard to remind self? Can God deal with death? I told the woman so. Can God deal with debt? I ventured as much with the man. Can God hear yet one more confession from these lips? The face in the mirror asks.

I sit a few feet from a man on death row. Jewish by birth. Tentmaker by trade. Apostle by calling. His days are marked. I'm curious about what bolsters this man as he nears his execution. So I ask some questions.

Do you have family, Paul? *I have none.*

What about your health? *My body is beaten and tired.*

What do you own? *I have my parchments. My pen. A cloak.*

And your reputation? *Well, it's not much. I'm a heretic to some, a maverick to others.*

Do you have friends? *I do, but even some of them have turned back.*

Any awards? *Not on earth.*

Then what do you have, Paul? No belongings. No family. Criticized by some. Mocked by others. What do you have, Paul? What do you have that matters?

I sit back quietly and watch. Paul rolls his hand into a fist. He looks at it. I look at it. What is he holding? What does he have?

He extends his hand so I can see. As I lean forward, he opens his fingers. I peer at his palm. It's empty.

I have my faith. It's all I have. But it's all I need. I have kept the faith.

Paul leans back against the wall of his cell and smiles. And I lean back against another and stare into the face of a man who has learned that there is more to life than meets the eye.

For that's what faith is. Faith is trusting what the eye can't see.

Eyes see the prowling lion. Faith sees Daniel's angel.

Eyes see storms. Faith sees Noah's rainbow.

Eyes see giants. Faith sees Canaan.

Your eyes see your faults. Your faith sees your Savior.

Your eyes see your guilt. Your faith sees his blood.

Your eyes see your grave. Your faith sees a city whose builder and maker is God.

Your eyes look in the mirror and see a sinner, a failure, a promise-breaker. But by faith you look in the mirror and see a robed prodigal bearing the ring of grace on your finger and the kiss of your Father on your face.

But wait a minute, someone asks. How do I know this is true? Nice prose, but give me the facts. How do I know these aren't just fanciful hopes?

Part of the answer can be found in Sara's little leaps of faith. Her older sister, Andrea, was in the room watching, and I asked Sara if she would jump to Andrea. Sara refused. I tried to convince her. She wouldn't budge. "Why not?" I asked.

"I only jump to big arms."

If we think the arms are weak, we won't jump.

For that reason, the Father flexed his muscles. "God's power is very great for those who believe," Paul taught. "That power is the same as the great strength God used to raise Christ from the dead" (Ephesians 1:19–20).

Next time you wonder if God can catch you, read that verse. The very arms that defeated death are the arms awaiting you.

Next time you wonder if God can forgive you, read that verse. The very hands that were nailed to the cross are open for you.

And the next time you wonder if you will survive the jump, think of Sara and me. If a flesh-and-bone-headed dad like me can catch his child, don't you think your eternal Father can catch you?

OUR FATHER WHO ART ON EARTH

CATHERINE MARSHALL

from *The Best of Catherine Marshall,*
edited by Leonard E. LeSourd

One of my favorite stories is about how Dad went down to the railroad yards near our home in Keyser, West Virginia, to seek out a new member of his congregation. In one of the Baltimore and Ohio's enormous roundhouses, the Reverend Wood found his man at work.

"Can't shake hands with you," said the man apologetically. "They're too grimy."

John Wood reached down to the ground and rubbed his hands in coal soot.

"How about it now?" he said, offering an equalized hand.

But if at an early age I knew I could trust my earthly father, I continued to resist the sermons that urged us to surrender our lives to a faraway God. What would that mean? The idea of spending all my time praying, reading the Bible, and talking about God did not appeal to me at all.

When the evangelist Gypsy Smith, Jr., came to hold services in our town, I went with curiosity but little more. A huge tent was pitched on a vacant lot near the town limits—not large enough to hold the crowds that flocked there. On a platform of raw wood from which the resin still oozed sat the massed choirs gathered from all the churches. Their favorite anthem was the spirited "Awakening Chorus":

> The Lord Jehovah reigns, and sin is backward hurled.
> Rejoice! Rejoice! Rejoice!

The "rejoicings" vibrated so shrilly that they raised goosebumps along my spine. As the congregation sang, the waving arms of the music director beat out the rhythms of hymns like

Standing on the prom-i-ses of Christ, my King . . .

or

Sing them o-ver a-gain to me,
Won-der-ful words of life . . .

Each time we collectively took a breath, the pianist would run in scales, chords, and flourishes marvelous to my childish ears.

Then came the preaching, so dynamic that decades later Gypsy Smith's thundering word-pictures still reverberate in my ears. Samson, succumbing to fleshly temptation, delivered into the hands of the Philistines, his hair cut, his eyes cruelly blinded. Then that final scene in Samson's drama where a repentant Samson, his hair grown back, faces three thousand Philistines gathered in the great hall to make sport of him. With his right hand on one of the two key pillars supporting the roof, his left hand on the other, Samson bows himself with all his might. . . .

The emotion in Gypsy's preaching, mounting steadily, transferred itself to the congregation. What did Samson's story have to do with Keyser, West Virginia? Selfishness and sensuality brought only destruction, the evangelist thundered. It would always be so. Each of us had to decide which road we would travel.

Finally a hush would fall over the tent as the choirs sang almost in a whisper,

Softly and tenderly Jesus is calling,
calling for you and for me . . .

Soon, at the far edge of the tent, someone would rise and make his way slowly down the aisle toward the front. Then another person, and another, and another. . . .

What impressed me were the faces of the people who went forward. There was radiance and joy on those faces. Most seemed eager to get to the front, where they knelt and wept and prayed and "gave themselves."

At home I asked my parents about the people who had made this act of commitment to God.

"Does this mean they joined the church?" I asked.

I wondered, too: Had not some of them "gone forward" out of the emotionalism of the moment?

Dad understood my wonderings behind the questions. Wisely he answered, "Sure, most of them will join a church. You, too, will want to do that at the right time. But Catherine, joining the church is only the outward part of it. You should not join the church until it really means something. It must mean the gift of yourself to God."

I pondered that statement many times during those preteen years.

I was nine on the Sunday morning when I sat in church beside my mother—my brother and sister were in Sunday school classes—and watched my father conduct the service. My heart was full of love for him in a special way. I can never remember many things he said from the pulpit, but I felt God's love flowing through him for all of us in the congregation.

At the end of the service, rather spontaneously as I recall, Dad issued an invitation for those to come forward who wanted to accept Jesus as the Lord of their lives and to be part of the church fellowship.

And suddenly I felt a stirring inside me. Very gentle. There was no voice, no words, just a feeling of great warmth. I loved my father dearly. And I trusted him with all my heart. I loved him so much that I could feel tears forming behind my eyes.

And then came the assurance. All along God had meant for the love of my earthly father to be a pattern of my heavenly Father and to show me the way to make connection with Him.

Following this inner conviction came the sudden urge to act and the will to do it. To my surprise and Mother's, I rose from the pew and walked down the aisle to the front, joining a half-dozen or so others.

At first Dad did not see me as the group formed a semicircle around the altar. He spoke to us briefly about the step we were taking and was about to pray when he noticed me.

Full recognition flashed into his brown eyes; he knew instantly that my being there was significant. I was presenting the gift of myself, a first step in faith. The resistance to surrender had been broken.

I shall never forget the look on my father's face. Surprise . . . joy . . . sudden vulnerability. He stood for a long moment in front of the altar, looking at me with eyes swimming in tears behind his spectacles. Then he pulled himself together and had us kneel as he prayed.

It was my first encounter with the living God—my heavenly Father. The catechism had said that He had loved me first. So had my earthly father. He must have loved me even before birth while I was carried in my mother's body.

Not only that, but since I could love and trust my earthly father, how much more could I love and trust my Father in heaven, and without fear place my future in His hands?

THE TRANSFORMATION
A PARABLE BY WAYNE HOLMES

"Why must I die?" she asked her father.

"Everything dies. But as I have tried to explain before, it's not really a death, but a transformation. There's more to you than what you are and what you have experienced, but first you must be willing to end this existence before you can enter into your new world—a world you will see from a whole new perspective."

"But I'm so young. I don't want to change. Besides, I'm afraid of the dark."

"Oh, little one, you worry so much. Haven't I told you many times before? The darkness is only temporary. Yes, you have lived for only a short time, but you have lived well. As for change, it's an inevitable part of life. Nothing stays the same. All of creation experiences change. To never change is to never experience life, and so it becomes a form of death. Welcome change as you would welcome a long lost love."

"But our customs are so barbaric. Why must we willingly participate in our death, and why must we build our own tombs?"

"It is our way. It has always been our way. I don't understand the reasons, but I know it's essential. Little one, this is your time. You have grown and you have learned your lessons well. Now it is time to enter a new realm of existence. Do not look upon this experience as an end, but look upon it as an entrance into a new dimension. View it as a door."

"Will I look the same, Father? Will you be able to recognize me?"

"No, my child, you will not look the same, but have no fear, a father can always recognize his child. You will be more beautiful than ever before. Your transformation will set your spirit free. You will no longer be confined by the restraints of this life, but you will be able to soar to new heights."

"What about love? Does this new life know of love?"

"Above all else, you will know of love. Because the spirit that is set free is the only spirit that can truly love and be loved to the depths of its being. It's a difficult thing that is asked of you, but it is in your own best interest, and it is my love for you that implores you to take this leap of faith."

––––––––

Knowing she was loved, and that she would also know love in her new world, she laid her questions to rest. She wondered why she was even worried to begin with. It wasn't as if she were hanging onto the greatest of lives anyway. She was considered repulsive and slow. No one cherished her company.

She went about her business as usual. Soon she would begin preparing for her transformation, as her father called it. It seemed like darkness and death to her. But she would participate like all those who went before her. She was who she was, and nothing could change that.

As a matter of fact, she actually began looking forward to her new life. *After all,* she reasoned, *there's nothing really special about being a caterpillar.*

BLESSED ASSURANCE

CHARLOTTE E. MERTZ

When I was very young, not yet in school, my family lived in the seaport city of St. John's, Newfoundland. The houses on our street, like most in the city, were constructed of wood and built with narrow passageways between them. Nights were damp and chilly. Houses were heated with coal fires that periodically spat glowing shards past the brick hearthstones onto the ancient wooden floors. Both chimney fires and house fires were common.

One evening we heard the clang of fire engines on our street. My family gathered outside to watch the excitement. Many of the neighbors were already standing about in the street to monitor the activity. Dad perched me high on his shoulders so I could see over the heads of the others who had come to watch. The air was filled with smoke and fog. The odors of woodsmoke and fishing boats were carried on the bone-chilling ocean breeze. Voices, shouts, sirens, bells—the cacophony was confusing and scary to a child. I could see it from the height of a man, but could understand it only from the experience of a child.

Fire rapidly consumed a house halfway down the block from ours. Flames shot high into the air—hot and orange and frightening. They reflected eerily off the fog that had rolled in across the harbor as the sun dropped below the horizon. Sparks spewed like fireworks into the heavy air and landed on nearby roofs, while firemen and the property owners soaked the shingles the best they could with hoses and buckets of water. The men did what they could to save the adjacent buildings, but the burning house was lost.

I huddled close to my father's head and wrapped my arms around his neck. I never doubted that my dad would keep me safe. The cold wind behind us and the blaze before us made me shiver. Most of all, I was overwhelmed.

Dad lifted me down to enfold me in his arms. "It's all right," he assured me. "The flames won't reach our house."

The likelihood that our house might burn had never occurred to me. But as this new and terrible possibility sank in, I began to sob with fear. Even at that young age, I realized that my fear didn't make sense: My father was there. Though the whole city should burn down around us, our house would be safe: Dad said so. We would be safe: He'd told me so. He would continue to shield me from the wind at our backs and the fire in our faces.

I continued to cry, and I buried my face against him. It was comforting to feel him hold me so close. He understood my fear. He gently held me there in his arms, till at last he carried me home.

Many times since then I have felt overwhelmed by circumstances far beyond my control. But God seems to lift me up onto his shoulders so I can see things from his perspective. I still perceive it with my limited human understanding, but I am assured that my Father sees it all. Wars, hatred, injustice, and illness are all beyond my understanding. They frighten me. Will they reach my land, my city, my home? Yet when I huddle close to my heavenly Father, I sense the shield he sets around me. He understands and knows it all. He's in control. With him, I'm safe, because he says so.

"It's all right," he seems to tell me. "The flames of hell will never reach you now." I believe him. Yet sometimes I'm still afraid. People around me struggle to save floundering marriages; some throw up their hands in despair as they watch their families dissolve. Could that happen to me? Like the fearful child I once was, I sometimes cry out for help. Then I feel his hand on me, comforting, protecting me from the terrors of this world. I see the glare of the threatening blaze. I feel the piercing wind. But my Father's here. I'll be all right. And he'll carry me safely home.

BEGINNING THE REAL RACE

LEIGHTON FORD

from *Sandy: A Heart for God*

Time, they say, heals. Time also sets ambushes. On a cold, clear Carolina afternoon, driving by Myers Park High School, memories suddenly come flooding back.

I stop, park, walk around the track where he ran so many races. It's nearly seven years since Sandy ran his last race, over three years since he left us.

Passing the starting line, I wish he could start his whole life again. But would we want him back if it meant going through all the pain and hurt?

Suppose God had come to us and said, "You can have Sandy. Here is what he is going to be like, but you can have him for only twenty-one years!" What would we have chosen? No question. We would take him again—and again. But when you love deeply, you hurt deeply.

Nobody could have told me three years ago how much we would miss him or for how long. There is nothing quite like the death of a child. I guess most folks think that in a few weeks or in a few months the pain is over. Maybe for some people. But not for me. Not for Jeanie.

I want so much to see him again. Watch his flying feet going around the track. See him duck his head in a moment of embarrassment. Watch him touch the corner between his eyes and his nose when he is thinking. See him pray, legs apart, long fingers pressing together, moving them up and down or pulling them apart when he can't get the right word. But the pain of death is its finality. Things are never the same again.

And yet they have gotten better. We can talk more freely about Sandy now. As a family we can laugh at his foibles, remembering how spacey he could be. But still I find it hard to look at his picture. Deb can't read his journals. Jeanie's eyelids began having spasms three months after he died.

They are better but still not perfect. And still the questions come.

I walk around the final curve on the track, past the green wall with the sign, "Go Mustangs," past the scoreboard. I stop and look down at the spot twenty yards from the finish line where his legs began to wobble in that final race.

Why? What happened that day? Why did his heart run away again? Why did the doctors say he could run? Why did we let him run? Why was his heart flawed in the first place? Was it the German measles that Jeanie was exposed to when she was carrying Sandy that did it? And why was he not healed?

So many questions. So few answers. "Where is God, Mom?" Sandy said, during his last illness. "I don't feel him. I need to feel him." And we have felt the same thing.

When I prayed the day before his surgery I said, "God, be good to my boy." But he died. Was God good to him?

When we get down to it, I guess Jeanie put it right that last night, "Either there is a God and he is good, or there is no God."

Atheists might not have such a big problem. They could shrug off such events as fate. So life is meaningless and why does it matter how long anyone lives? It is all an accident anyway. And in that case, why do I love? Chemicals, loving chemicals.

How absurd!

But we did love him. And we do. And life is not nothing. So we choose to dwell, not on the pain of losing him, but on the wonder that we had him at all.

"When a good young man dies; what a waste, who can explain it?" That question headlined a newspaper story the Sunday after Sandy died. Many would say, "What a tragedy, his race was cut short." But that gives me pause. Is *tragic* a word that belongs in a Christian's vocabulary? Pain and suffering, yes, and loss and anguish and questioning. But *tragedy* is a word from the ancient Greeks not from the language of the Bible.

I have looked at a lot of Sandy's pictures since he died. And I have realized what a very great difference it makes whether I look at them from the viewpoint of life or of death.

Here is what I mean. When Sandy was physically alive and with us I would have looked at those pictures with more or less interest, regret or pride, with a sense of wonder at what he grew into.

Now, after his death, I look at each one with a little voice saying over my shoulder, "How tragic, that Sandy would only live until he was twenty-one."

It is the same way when I read his journal. I tend to read with a tragic sense that keeps murmuring, "And he only had six months, or one month, or one week to live."

How important then to decide what is Sandy's true end! If twenty-one years was the end, then it does seem tragic. (Then I must discover why it is tragic and not a meaningless event to be shrugged off. If there is nothing more, then there really is nothing ultimately important.)

But if eternity is his end, then I can look from his infancy to his manhood and see each part fitting into an eternal whole which is yet beyond my ken, but not my hope.

On the one view, death leads to the trash heap.

On the other, death is swallowed up in glory.

So as I think of the infant son who became our grown-up son, I can imagine him a man who has become a glorious creature of eternity.

Philosophizing, though, does not take away the pain that twists my insides when I think how achingly I miss him. But as Jeanie has reminded me, "We have got to see things from Sandy's perspective."

Was twenty-one years enough? Or would twenty-two have been enough? Or twenty-three? Or would it have taken seventy-three? Then why not seventy-four?

Isn't it what fills those years that matters? Is time just clock-time or opportunity-time—or God-time? Is it how long or how full? For Sandy, the cup of time was running over. God so filled those years that they are going to keep brimming over.

Right here somewhere along this track, he learned to pass the baton on to his teammates. He did it in life, he did it in death. I think of so many who have picked up the baton and have run on—Fran, Susan, Billy, Lisa, Kendall, Kevin.

The year after Sandy died, Kevin and I were raking leaves and talking about how we missed him. Kevin said, "But, Dad, maybe Sandy's influence has been far greater than if he had lived. His life was like a very bright light—a spotlight—focused intensely. But his death has been a floodlight. It has covered a much wider area."

Again, I have become convinced that John 12 is not just a metaphor but a literal truth. "Unless a grain of wheat falls into the ground and dies, it abides alone, but if it dies it brings forth many seeds."

Life blossoming from death. That is God's way. It is the way of the cross. And we have seen how God has taken characteristics of Sandy, godly traits, and placed them into the friends who loved him. More compassion into one. More commitment into another.

But not everybody has picked up the baton. Some of his friends have let it fall. Or took it and then stepped aside. "Is this what you get for following Christ—for pursuing God—to die young?" I can imagine some of them saying that.

"But what are the options?" I want to ask. "To be bad and die young? To be bad and die old? Or to be neutral and count for nothing?"

I guess what we would all like is to be good and have fun and die old. I wish with all my heart that could have been for Sandy. But it wasn't to be.

We have no regrets. No unsaid words we wished we had said. No desire that Sandy had been a different kind of person. At least, as someone said, Jeanie and I have "clean sorrow." Still, I want him. I want to see those pounding feet, the curly hair, the smile, the serious, thoughtful eyes. I want him to run not just here on the track but all through his life.

Yes, I believe God is good and strong and that he brings blessing out of pain. But I would be less than honest if I didn't acknowledge the part of me inside that says, "It is not right."

It is not right that Sandy is not coming home again. It is not right that he doesn't share the joys and triumphs of his brother's life, and of his sister's little son, Graham, who will only know Uncle Sandy by his picture. It is not right that he will not marry and have children. It is not right that he is not going to fulfill the ministry that we believe might have been there.

I sense these things inside myself and I ask, "Am I doubting God?"

But Sandy's death is *not* right. As Christians we sometimes too easily and glibly pass over things that happen with nice sweet words, and forget that it is not right.

I remember that our Lord stood at the grave of his friend, Lazarus. The Scripture says that he was "deeply troubled in his spirit" (John 11:33). The word taken literally means he "snorted" in his spirit like a warhorse facing battle, seeing what death and evil had done to the beautiful world his Father had made. And for a beautiful young man, it is not right.

We can't just gloss that over. I think that's what Paul meant in 1 Corinthians 15, when he stated, "The last enemy to be destroyed is death." Death is an enemy. The gospel is not a sugar coating to make a bitter pill taste better. The gospel is the difference between life and death. If Christ has not been raised, our faith is vain, and those who have died are gone forever. If only for this life we have hope in Christ, we are to be pitied. But Christ indeed has been raised from the dead and has become the firstfruits of those who have fallen asleep (1 Cor. 15:16–20).

Weeks after Sandy died, a letter came from the missionary under whose direction he worked that summer in France. He wrote, "We are so earthbound. We assume that the main part of God's will and work is here on earth. I believe that not only the best is yet to come, but the highest will also be there . . . *God never wastes anything* . . . rather than being the end, this is the Beginning!"

So I stand here on the track. With my toe, I draw a line where the finish line was, where Sandy finished his last race. But the finish line is also the starting line. And that is what makes the pain bearable. That is what undergirds the loss with hope. That is what makes the race worth running. Suppose that life is not the race. Suppose life is only the training season, and Eternity is the real race.

Then Sandy's heart was beating, not just for a medley relay, not just twenty-one years, but for eternity. The weight he carried—including a wounded heart—was preparing him for an eternal weight of glory.

Sometimes in my mind, I whisper, "What is it like, son?"

And I hear him say, "I can think so deeply and every thought is clear. I can speak and express exactly what I mean. I can run and never get tired. I am so surefooted in the paths of glory."

So a son leaves a legacy for a father. I have determined to run my race for Christ to the end. And when that time comes maybe our Savior will let him come running to meet me. Then with all sons and daughters of the resurrection, our hearts will beat and run for God forever.

THROUGH THE STORM

BOB MAHAFFEY

The ominous sky grew darker. Dad sat in the stern next to the outboard motor and jerked the cord to start the engine. A puff of exhaust brought the smell of gasoline. My dad pointed the bow of the craft in the direction he knew so well, toward the dock where our two-tone blue '63 Buick Special waited to take us to safety. I was nine years old, and although it's now been thirty-nine years, I still remember it as the day I thought I would die.

The day had started calmly enough at 3:00 A.M., when Pops (my dad) quietly woke me for a big day of fishing on Lake Tohopekaliga in Kissimmee, Florida. Mom and Grandma were also awake and had already prepared my favorite breakfast—strawberry shortcake with milk poured over it and a dash of sugar on top. I had kissed my mom good-bye, and now I wondered if I'd ever see her again.

That predawn calm was a stark contrast to the panic I now felt. The storm didn't creep up on us the way many storms do. This late afternoon downpour arrived full-blown right from the start. The wind howled around us, blowing with gale-force strength, creating waves capped with white spray. As our little boat roller-coastered over the waves, we were forced to shield our eyes from the blowing rain to see where we were going. There wasn't much to see, just sheets of rain, dark clouds, and rolling waves.

This wasn't a silent storm. Lightning bolts cracked open the sky, providing enough light for me to glimpse my father sitting calmly in the rear of the boat, only a few feet away. Seconds later I cringed as the thunder roared its angry reply. I don't know why the heavens were so mad that day, but the lightning, the thunder, the wind, and the waves were fighting each other. And we were caught in the middle.

I sat in that small, metal fishing boat, my bravery sloshed overboard. My fears brought large tears that blurred my already limited vision. The waves splashed over the small boat; at times I could see the bottom of the lake.

To me, the safest place would have been near my dad, sitting by his side with his arm around me. Cautiously, trying not to tip the boat, I crept closer to him from my seat in the front. But before I could reach him, I heard him shout over the blowing wind and crashing water, "Stay where you are!"

Immediately I stopped. I couldn't believe he didn't want me with him. I didn't understand my dad's reasoning. All I knew was, I didn't want to be alone in the front of the boat. *What can I hold on to?* I thought. *How long before I'm washed overboard?* I didn't know at the time he was only trying to keep the boat balanced. Slowly I made my way back to my seat. I was sure we would capsize. I would be lost from my dad, and I was certain we would die.

At times I could barely see Dad through the darkness and the pouring sheets of rain. When I did catch a glimpse of him, he appeared unfazed by the fierceness of the storm. Having been on the lake numerous times before, he knew what he was doing and where he was going. Through my tears I kept peering back to him. His gaze pierced forward. His care for me was matched by his ability to navigate the storm.

Two hours passed before the elements relented. The boat had taken on gallons of water, slowing our process even further. We had been on the lake for sixteen hours. The sun was setting when the most favorable scene came into view: the shoreline where my mother and grandparents stood watching and waiting for our safe return.

———

My father has been gone for several years. I'm grateful for my dad. Not only did he see me through that stormy day on Lake Tohopekaliga, but as I grew up he also saw me through many other turbulent times.

As much as I loved Dad, I also have another Father—one I love even more. This Father also rides with me, sitting at the controls, guiding me through life. When life's storms assault me and I'm tempted by fears that can paralyze in the crises of life, I remember that day on the lake. I know that my Father's view of the future, his perfect care, and his ability to lead me through the storms of life are all-sufficient.

I am blessed.

I have the memories of a wonderful dad whose loving protection taught me about the love and care of the Father.

Father God, thank you for Pops . . . and for seeing me through the storms of life.

SECTION *Seven*

The PROVISION
OF A FATHER

IN THE VERY HEART OF THE WORLD

MOTHER TERESA

from *Loving Jesus*,
edited by José Luis González-Balado

We, the missionaries of charity, have homes for the sick and dying in many places. We also have children's homes for the unwanted, the unloved, the sick, and the retarded.

God has been just wonderful to us by giving us more parents, especially in India, who want to adopt our children. We have many children ready to be adopted.

People very often make jokes with me (or about me, rather), because we are also teaching natural family planning. They say, "Mother Teresa is doing plenty of talking about family planning, but she herself does not practice it. She is having more and more children every day."

Indeed, that is the way it is. Our homes are always full of children. And as they come, God has been tremendously wonderful to us. We always get plenty of parents who are hungry to give their love and their home to a child. You would be surprised how much love is showered on those unwanted little children, who otherwise would have been destined to live in the gutter.

Lately, I have experienced what a child meant for the family that adopted him. I had given the child to a high-class family. After some time, I heard that the child was sick and completely crippled.

So I sent to the family and said, "Give the child back to me and I will give you a healthy one!"

The father said to me, "Take my life first, before you take this child!"

That shows you what the child meant to that family and how beautifully that little one, in spite of all his suffering, had fit into the lives of those people.

———————

Editor's Note: *There have been times in my life when I have felt sick and crippled, either physically, or mentally. The world, with all its evil intent, has left me lying in the gutter, despairing for life and love.*

Perhaps you have been there too.

Mother Teresa reminds us that we belong to the Father and that he loves us with an undying, unconditional love. We are his children. Give us back to the gutter of our humble existence? Never! In fact, he would rather die first.

As a matter of fact, he did just that.

JACK-OF-ALL-TRADES

KAREN BURTON MAINS

from *Friends and Strangers*

Thirteen years ago, within twelve months of moving into our home, we began to have problems with water damage. First the dormers in the front bedrooms leaked when there were hard rains. Then, during a winter of record-breaking snowfalls, the snow on the roof froze hard, impacting the ice-line, which turned to water within the attic when the ice met the warm air rising from inside the house. This resulted in some twenty different dripping leaks through the living room and dining room ceilings.

Insurance, of course, paid for this water damage, but the money went to pay a tuition bill that was also due.

Then the pipes in one of the upstairs bathrooms froze and a child (who shall remain nameless) unintentionally left his dry water faucet in the "on" position. When we returned from church that Sunday afternoon, the pipes had thawed. Water gushed over the sink, rushed along the floorboards, fell like a waterfall in the dining room, and then seeped down into the basement.

Later, a crack in the foundation resulted in water collecting in the northeast corner of the basement. When a sump pump gave out during spring storms, when the humidifier on the furnace went, when the drain in the laundry room sink plugged and overflowed during the washing machine spin cycles, more water collected—a lot more water. All of this water stained an indelible water line on the new rough cedar siding.

Why didn't we have all this fixed?

In self-defense, I can say that I have called plumbers. I've pleaded with roof men. Every one of them told me something must be done. All looked at the bows and waves in the plasterboard and said, "Lady, you're going to have to replace that whole ceiling before it tears off and falls on some-one's head." But then they just disappeared, never to be heard of again.

And truthfully, between tithes, taxes, and college tuitions, there just didn't seem to be enough money to go around so I didn't insist they return to do the work.

The leaks in my house have amounted to domestic Chinese water torture. I've prayed for years, tried to resign myself to the mess, looked in the other direction, but finally, on December 1, 1989, I was a discouraged lady.

I know this because I recorded my feelings in my prayer journal. "Fri-day, December 1, 1989," I wrote. "A bad day. Feeling emotionally dis-couraged."

Actually, I had had a bad year. The year 1989 had brought discour-aging news to many para-church ministries, our national broadcast, "The Chapel of the Air," included. Mail response, partly as a result of the televangelist scandals, had dropped drastically. Never before had we suf-fered such financial reversals. (And that is saying something, because The Chapel has rarely, underline rarely, been anything more than solvent.) David had been forced to cut $400,000 out of an already-trimmed 1990 budget. We dropped stations not paying for their own airtime in finan-cially stricken areas of the country, released long-term employees, reposi-tioned our entire work force in an attempt to cover responsibilities. We spent hours in prayer and days in fasting seeking the comfort and leading of the Lord.

Keeping vigil over a ministry in what might be its death throes (and with the only words from the Lord regarding the future being "Trust me") forces painful self-questioning upon the ministry's leaders. And on Friday, December 1, 1989, I was weary of hoping, weary of fighting off anxiety, exhausted from self-examination, and dumbfounded as to how to pray. ("All prayed-out!" is a family expression that described my state.) Despite my Christian walk, I was simply unable to trust that the Lord Almighty was doing His good work in our lives.

What did I want? I asked myself. Not very much. I just wanted enough financial bread for each day for The Chapel of the Air year. I didn't need us to be contenders for the largest, most successful media ministry. I didn't expect broad and rapid expansion of listener outlets. I didn't want the newest, biggest buildings, or state-of-the-art recording studios. I just wanted enough to pay this day's bills and make up the horrendous debt, some $750,000 worth, which had accumulated since the scandal-filled summer of 1989.

Oh, it was a bad day that first day of December. My journal records four more short items of "what I wanted." The last reads: "I'd be perfectly content with my personal material life if only the leaks in the ceilings of our home were repaired." In more candid terms that meant: "And oh, by the way, God, if You're so great; if You've promised to take care of all our needs, why don't You do something simple. Fix the leaks in the ceiling, for instance! I've been praying about that a long time."

Miraculously (and I mean that), by December 22, 1989, the living room and dining room ceilings had been torn out, the leaks located and repaired, and new plasterboard mounted and taped. How did all this happen?

A young man we had never met, a pastor who had just resigned and was between jobs, walked into David's office and said: "I don't have funds to help you in your financial crisis, but I know I wouldn't have made it through this last year without your radio broadcast. I do have construction skills. Is there anything I can do along that line?"

And like the Little Red Hen, he did. He surveyed our house, sighed, then took on the largest, messiest, most difficult of the neglected jobs. He carried out the furniture to the garage or stacked it in the bedrooms. He unfastened the chandelier from its electrical connection, ripped out the moldering dry wall, removed toilets (and since they were out, replaced them), tore up the flooring in the bathroom, located leaks, repaired leaks, laid new tile of my choice, grouted the tubs, and mounted fresh plasterboard.

All this for a grand total of $234.31. My benefactor wrote my bill out on stationery imprinted with a heading that read:

JACK-OF-ALL-TRADES
General Home Repairs
Painting, Carpentry, Plumbing, Roofing

His charges were for materials. His labor: $00.00.

Let us not investigate the peculiar theology of an angry, discouraged woman before her God. Let me instead praise the great gift this young man gave to me. First of all, there was the work, the repair itself; David and I could never have afforded to pay for this labor. As needful as it was, it was beyond our financial means. That was the obvious gift.

But just as the drip damage was a symbol of our greater problem—a ministry leaking away thousands upon thousands of dollars—the act of this man accumulated deeper levels of meaning for me.

David is not a Mr. Fix-It. He grew up in a family that hired out household repairs. In my family, my dad (when he could get around to it) fixed everything from cars to sinks to washing machines.

This was wonderful to me. It established in my mind the idea: *Dad can take care of it.* When he found time from his duties as the head of the Music Department at Moody Bible Institute, Dad would make it right. (The shadow of this is that we had four castoff automatic washers collected in the basement for extra parts—just in case.) One of the wonderful experiences of my childhood was watching Dad make things work. Sometimes, we children were invited to help him.

One of my dad's favorite do-it-yourself measures solved the problem of clogged drains. He would run a garden hose from the outside spigot through an open window into the house, plunge it down the clogged drain, turn on the pressure, and flush out the line.

He was a sublimely pragmatic handyman. Once, the line from the outside sewer backed up, gnarled with tree roots. This required that we rent an electric router from a nearby plumbing supply. Dad lifted the sewer cap and started to use the router, but he found that the line didn't slip into the L in the pipe going out to the street. So Dad lowered me—wrists clasped to wrists—down into the sewer where I could feed the line into the sewer conduit, taking the play out of the twisting contraption.

When a parent is alive who can make things work, a child feels as though chaos can be kept at bay. My father always calmed me by beginning his explanations with, "Now Sweet . . . now Sweet, what seems to be the trouble?"

After his death I felt his loss in many ways, and one of them was most certainly his absence in times of minor domestic crises. There was no one to be a father to me now. No one to make it work, to know how to fix it. No one to call and whine, "Dad, this stupid sink's backed up again!" Or, "The boys flushed their plastic soldiers down the toilets!"

Jack-Of-All-Trades could do the things my dad had been able to do. His help made me feel that I was cared for, protected. He could even pass on the wisdom of carpentry and tools to my children. My third son, Joel, was home on his winter break from college when Jack-Of-All-Trades tore out my ceiling. For much of the time, they worked in tandem. See, this is the way you remove a toilet. This is the way you use a cordless drill. This is the way you lay a sub-floor. This is the way you drop a plumb line. This is the way you measure out tile. This is how you put up dry wall. This is how you tape, prime, and paint a new ceiling. Unasked-for gifts now given.

Most importantly, this gift of a stranger put me back to rights again with my God. I understood very clearly by the timing of this answer to prayer, that the divine Mr. Fix-it—upon whom I was more obviously forced to depend after the death of my father—was saying: *Now Sweet, now Sweet, what seems to be the matter? I am perfectly able to answer your prayers in ways that are unfathomable to you. But the timing must be mine. When the time is right and when the way is right, I can bring all things about.* And that is the fixing I most deeply needed.

THE WAY THEY WERE
RUTH BELL GRAHAM

from *It's My Turn*

S peaking of giants, when Daddy and Mother landed in Shanghai in 1916 (Daddy, fresh out of the Medical College of Virginia in Richmond, and twenty-two years old), Mother was a slim 114 pounds. "Poor little Virginia Bell!" one missionary is reported to have exclaimed. "She won't last a year!"

She fooled them. She not only lasted a year—she lasted twenty-five of them before returning to the States to live another thirty-three.

She built a house, had three children, buried one, had two more, taught her children at home through the fifth grade, ran the women's clinic, always had another missionary or two in the home, planned the menus, taught the cook how to prepare American food, checked accounts with him daily, examined each piece of linen as it came back from the hospital laundry to make sure no bedbugs were hiding in the folds, entertained often and well, and wrote home faithfully.

In the evenings she saw to it that we played games together or that we "womenfolk" did handwork (knitting, embroidery, braiding rugs, crocheting, and sewing) while the men took turns reading aloud books ranging from Dickens, *Uncle Remus, Ben-Hur*, to Sir Walter Scott. Evenings were family times for us.

Daddy was the head of the surgical work in the hospital. Dr. James B. Woods directed the medical work. They believed the hospital existed primarily for the preaching of the Gospel. A full-time evangelist was employed to minister to the men patients, and a Bible woman to the women. Gospel tracts were given not only to the patients but to the families who, according to local custom, accompanied them to the hospital.

This did not mean that Daddy and Dr. Woods did not run a tight ship. They developed a hospital that the American Medical Association eventually recognized as qualified for the training of interns from this country. And on his fortieth birthday, Daddy was made a Fellow of the American College of Surgeons.

Daddy was a man's man: an athlete, a daredevil, a practical jokester. He loved music, played the guitar, and had a fine singing voice. He laughed heartily and found much to laugh over. He was also known as a hard worker, moving quickly and surely through life as if he always knew where he was going and what God would have him do.

And I'm sure he did, for I cannot recall getting up in the morning but what Daddy would be reading his Bible (and his greeting, "Ruth, have you read your Bible yet?" frequently sent me back to my room to begin the day as I should), or on his knees getting his instructions from God.

Those instructions were always practical and down-to-earth, which is, after all, where Daddy lived.

The following incident illustrates just how very down-to-earth he could be.

One night we were driving through the narrow streets of Tsingkiang, approximately 250 miles north of Shanghai, in Kiangsu Province.

It was summertime and the isinglass flaps which served as windows in the little British Austin were off.

Progress through the narrow, stone-paved streets was slow and precarious because it was both sidewalk and street, and packed with people. Along with the occasional rickshaw, and the barrow men carefully balancing their heavily loaded wheelbarrows, trotted the bucket bearers, carrying pungent night soil balanced at each end of the *biendan* across their shoulders. Occasionally, the car had to come to a full stop while some merchant pulled his wares back into his shop in order to make room for us to pass.

It was at a point when the car had come almost to a standstill that a young boy, peering in along with scores of other Chinese to see the "foreign devils," took full advantage of the situation and let loose with a well-aimed mouthful of spit. The car moved just slightly and, missing Daddy, it landed *splat!* right on me.

Daddy slammed on the brakes and bolted out the door. The culprit, sensing disaster, took off through the crowd as fast as his legs could carry him. But Daddy, in his earlier days purchased as a pitcher by the Baltimore Orioles, was no mean athlete himself, and while the little boy had size on his side, Daddy had determination on his.

Back through the narrow streets they tore, the crowd parting to let them pass, some people startled, others amused, realizing, no doubt, that the "foreign devil" had good reason for what he was doing.

Through the eastern gate of the mud wall they went, up onto the narrow-gauge railroad track (on which I never saw a train), and down the tracks, until finally Daddy overtook the culprit, turned him over his knee, and spanked him soundly.

What a man!

––––––

Editor's Note: *There have been times in my life when I felt as if the world was spitting on me. Usually, these times are the result of personal insult. Someone has felt it was their responsibility to offer their opinion in an unfriendly manner. At times like these, God, my heavenly Father, comes to my aid. He wipes away the spit and tells me not to worry—everything will be all right.*

But, there are other times when God seems to race from the scene, leaving me in my shame to wonder where he has gone and why he has deserted me. Often it is not until some time later that I discover he has taken it upon himself to discipline my accuser. In one way or another, he has administered a spiritual spanking to the one who sought to do me harm. "It is mine to avenge; I will repay," says the Lord (Hebrews 10:30). And you know what? He does! In his way and in his time, he does!

What a God!

DADDY IS AWAKE

PHIL CALLAWAY

from *Who Put the Skunk in the Trunk?*

There are moments when everything goes well; don't be frightened, it won't last.   —Jules Renard

When I was a boy of eight or nine, my parents saw fit to give me a room of my very own far removed from the rest of the family, in a rather dark area at the south end of our house. I'm sure they thought they were doing me a big favor by putting me there. After all, a boy with some space of his own is a happy boy, a well-adjusted, confident child, ready to face the world. But parents can't be right about everything.

For a boy of eight or nine there was much to be afraid of in those days, even outside that shadowy room. My older brother David cared much about my well being, and so he made sure I was aware of certain dangers that came along with living in the Great White North. For instance, icicles were a concern. A twenty-four-pounder with a razor-sharp point could do significant damage to a third-grader's complexion if he slammed the door too hard and looked up on his way to school some January morning. It's not a pretty sight, a child pinned to a snowdrift in that manner.

And then there were the bears. Grizzly bears. According to my brother, a whole tribe of them lived just beyond the trees out back of our house. Big furry ones. If you stayed awake long enough you could hear them growling late at night. Sometimes their leader, Vicious Vince, would growl mournfully, a sure sign that the tribe had not eaten in a while. And that Vince's cavities were bothering him.

"What do they eat?" I asked, proving that the person who said there are no dumb questions had not made my acquaintance.

"Oh, they like nothing better than small boys . . . they start with the arms."

"How come I ain't heard of no one being eaten?"

"They don't leave any evidence. They even eat the bones. And no one wants to talk about it. Remember Tom, that freckled kid in your class last year?"

"Yeah."

"Well, where do you think he went?"

I didn't know, I had to admit, as my eyes grew wider. And each morning on my way to school, I shut the door carefully and tiptoed through those trees like a soldier behind enemy lines.

On the afternoon of the day I took up residency in my new room, we watched a film at school. It was called *Mary, Queen of Scots*, and I suppose our teacher must have left the room after she wound up the projector, because the film was intended for a much more mature audience than third-graders.

It was the true story of a queen who was married at fifteen to a man with whom she never quite saw eye-to-eye, judging from the fact that she blew him up with gunpowder in a memorable scene midway through the movie. But the final frames were far more memorable. Sentenced to death, Mary had her head covered with a dark cloth. Standing over her with an axe, a rather muscular man severed that cloth from the rest of her then dumped it with great ceremony in a wooden box.

We watched all this in black-and-white, which for some reason only heightened the terror. Black-and-white films spoke of history, of accuracy, of finality. Certain boys in our class seemed to enjoy the film immensely, and on the surface, I seemed to be one of them. But as we filed quietly from the film room that afternoon, I knew deep down in my stomach that I would not sleep a wink until I was a teenager. And after school, I asked a friend to walk home with me so I could show him my race car set.

That night after the lights dimmed, I lay in bed watching my wall for strange shadows and listening carefully for strange noises. Neither were hard to find. I could hear a man creeping down the hallway toward me, dragging an ax behind him. The floorboards creaked. The bears growled mournfully. I pulled the covers higher. It was tough knowing how high to pull them. Should you completely cover your head? Or would you rather be aware of what takes place during the final seconds of your life? The hooded creature above you. The ax swinging down. I wondered how long it took for an eight-year-old's life to flash before him.

Suddenly . . . the sound of footsteps. This was not my imagination.

My entire body froze stiff, every nerve ending on alert. The footsteps drew closer. Looming in the doorway was a shadow, one hand on its throat, the other thrashing wildly toward me. The shadow growled: "Aaaaahhh!"

I lay stiff, unable to move, clutching my tiny chest and gurgling.

My brother David stood in the doorway, laughing, as if a heart attack was the funniest thing he could imagine me having.

I slumped and lay still, my eyes wide open. David's smile began to wrinkle and he reached down to shake me. "You okay?" he asked, genuinely concerned.

I didn't move.

It was the only revenge I could think of.

For some reason David seemed to treat me nicer after that. Brought me things. Gave me an underduck on the swing set without telling me I would never come down. And on the following Monday afternoon, I came home from school to find him eating a Snickers bar. He even offered me the last half.

That very same day Mother hung two plaques neatly beside my bed. They seemed to share a common theme and though I wasn't the sharpest knife in the drawer, I knew what the theme was.

The Lord is my light and my salvation—
whom shall I fear?
The Lord is the stronghold of my life—
of whom shall I be afraid? . . .
When my enemies and my foes attack me,
they will stumble and fall.
    —Psalm 27:1–3

So do not fear, for I am with you;
do not be dismayed,
for I am your God.
I will strengthen you and help you;
I will uphold you with my righteous right hand.
For I am the Lord, your God,
who takes hold of your right hand
and says to you, Do not fear; I will help you.
    —Isaiah 41:10, 13

I would love to tell you that I dealt with all my fears that day. That as I memorized those Scripture verses, thoughts of bears and axes and icicles melted into peace, and I began to snore . . . smiling. I would love to tell you that ever since then my life has been one long stretch of fearless living, marked by victory over the concerns that face us all.

The truth is, it would take three decades and an eight-year-old of my own to teach me why we have every reason to trust, and no need to fear.

"Daddy . . ."

It is midnight. A small girl in socked feet stands in our bedroom doorway silhouetted by the soft glow of a night-light. "Daddy . . . I'm scared."

It is the third time we've covered this territory tonight. I take her hand and pull back her covers. Beside her bed hang the same two verses that once framed mine.

"Rachael," I say, "did you go over your Bible verses?"

"Yup."

"And you counted sheep?"

"Yup."

"And you talked to the Shepherd?"

"Uh-huh."

"Hmm . . . well, I want to tell you a secret. Something I hope you'll never forget."

"What's that?"

"Well, you see . . . some people seem to need more sleep than others. And I'm one of those who doesn't sleep as much as you. Have you ever knocked on my door late at night and found me sleeping?"

"Um . . . nope."

"So if a burglar comes, I'll be awake, right?"

"Uh-huh."

"And if a monster ever comes to visit, he can find me just around the corner, can't he?"

"Uh-huh."

"Then go to sleep, Rachael . . . Daddy is awake."

I kiss her forehead then. And her nose. And her dimpled chin. "I love you, sweetheart."

"Love you too, Daddy."

A few minutes later I tiptoe from her room and climb into my own bed, resting ice-cold feet on the back of my wife's leg.

She sits straight up. "Italian dressing?" she says groggily, then lies back down. And I go to sleep with a very satisfied smile stuck to my face.

It's easy to rest in peace when you know that your Father is awake.

NO ODDBALLS
ALLOWED

PHILIP D. YANCEY

from *What's So Amazing About Grace?*

In this day, when tribalism sparks massacres in Africa, when nations redraw boundaries based on ethnic background, when racism in the United States mocks our nation's great ideals, when minorities and splinter groups lobby for their rights, I know of no more powerful message of the gospel than this, the message that got Jesus killed. The walls separating us from each other, and from God, have been demolished. We're all oddballs, but God loves us anyhow.

Almost twenty centuries have passed since God enlightened the apostle Peter on a rooftop. In that time, many circumstances have changed (no one is worrying about de-Judaizing the church anymore). Yet the shift that Jesus introduced has important consequences for every Christian. Jesus' revolution of grace affects me deeply in at least two ways.

First, it affects my access to God. In the same church service in which Bill Leslie divided our sanctuary into the approximate proportions of the Jewish temple, members of the congregation acted out a skit. Several petitioners approached the platform to deliver a message to the priest—with the women, of course, relying on their male representatives. Some brought sacrifices for the priest to present to God. Others made specific requests: "Could you talk to God about my problem?" they asked. Each time the "priest" would mount the platform, go through a prescribed ritual, and submit the request to God inside the Most Holy Place.

Suddenly, in the midst of this ceremony, a young woman came running down the aisle, disregarding the boundary set for her gender, with a Bible open to the book of Hebrews. "Hey, any of us can talk to God directly!" she proclaimed. "Listen to this."

Therefore, since we have a great high priest who has gone through the heavens, Jesus the Son of God, let us hold firmly to the faith we profess. . . . Let us then approach the *throne of grace* with confidence.

"And here it is again,"

. . . since we have confidence to enter the Most Holy Place by the blood of Jesus, by a new and living way opened for us through the curtain, that is, his body, and since we have a great priest over the house of God, let us draw near to God. . . .

"Any of us can enter the Most Holy Place!" she said before running offstage. "Any of us can come to God directly!"

In his sermon, the pastor spoke of the remarkable change of "God drawing near." You need only read the book of Leviticus and then turn to Acts to sense the seismic change. Whereas Old Testament worshipers purified themselves before entering the temple and presented their offerings to God through a priest, in Acts God's followers (good Jews, most of them) were meeting in private homes and addressing God with the informal *Abba*. It was a familiar term of family affection, like "Daddy," and before Jesus no one would have thought of applying such a word to Yahweh, the Sovereign Lord of the Universe. After him, it became the standard word used by early Christians to address God in prayer.

Earlier, I drew a parallel of a visitor in the White House. No such visitor, I said, could expect to barge into the Oval Office to see the President without an appointment. There are exceptions. During John F. Kennedy's administration, photographers sometimes captured a winsome scene. Seated around the President's desk in gray suits, cabinet members are debating matters of world consequence, such as the Cuban missile crisis. Meanwhile, a toddler, the two-year-old John-John, crawls atop the huge Presidential desk, oblivious to White House protocol and the weighty matters of state. John-John was simply visiting his daddy, and sometimes to his father's delight he would wander into the Oval Office with nary a knock.

That is the kind of shocking accessibility conveyed in Jesus' word *Abba*. God may be the Sovereign Lord of the Universe, but through his Son, God has made himself as approachable as any doting human father. In Romans 8, Paul brings the image of intimacy even closer. God's Spirit lives inside us, he says, and when we do not know what we ought to pray "the Spirit himself intercedes for us with groans that words cannot express."

We need not approach God by a ladder of hierarchy, anxious about cleanliness issues. If God's kingdom had a "No Oddballs Allowed" sign posted, none of us could get in. Jesus came to demonstrate that a perfect and holy God welcomes pleas for help from a widow with two mites and from a Roman centurion and a miserable publican and a thief on a cross. We need only call out "Abba" or, failing that, simply groan. God has come that close.

BLUE STONES
CAN HURT!

CORRIE TEN BOOM

from *In My Father's House*

School life did not prove to be as horrible as I thought. I can still remember the sensation of victory when I worked an arithmetic problem and discovered that the final figure was what it was supposed to be. However, my mind was not always so attentive to details. I was a daydreamer, carrying my fantasies into a world where everyone needed an expensive new watch, and every day was a walk on the dunes with the sunshine warming my cheeks.

The headmaster of our school was a strict taskmaster, insisting upon obedience and discipline without question. He had warned all the children not to step on the "blue stone," which was a small square stone slightly higher than the rest in the outer yard. I was not paying attention to his instructions and stepped on the stone. Instantly my face was smarting from a sharp slap on my cheek. I can still feel the shame of it, after all these years, for I don't believe the people at home had ever slapped my face. A color photoplate was impressed upon my mind, which has never faded. The tears covered my face, but I could see the girl who stood in front of me who wore a red dress and a white apron; there was a green door on the garden gate, and the colors all blended with the blazing eyes of Mr. Loran, the headmaster.

I couldn't wait to get home that day. Before I opened the door my cries had overpowered the sound of the bell, which announced any visitors to the shop.

Mama took me on her lap and comforted me; and when I had quieted, Papa held me in his arms as he did when I was a baby. I can still feel the sensation of safety as I put my head upon his shoulder. What a security to have a refuge when life is really hard!

Forty-five years passed after the blue-stone incident. The gestapo had arrested me, and I was being asked the location of the secret room in which I had hidden four Jews and two underground workers. I realized that if I told, it would mean prison and possibly death for the six people who were there, so I didn't tell. The interrogator slapped me on the face, and at the same moment I recalled the backyard of the school, the angry headmaster, and Mother and Father's comforting help.

"Lord Jesus, cover me!" I cried.

"If you mention that name, I'll murder you!" shouted the man. But his hand stopped in midair and he couldn't beat me any longer.

What a security to have a refuge when life is really hard.

SECTION Eight

The COMFORT
OF A FATHER

A ROOTED LIFE

JIMMY CARTER

from *Living Faith*

My father had also taught me what it means to live under strict discipline. Sometimes I was deeply resentful when he punished me, but I knew where I stood, what was expected of me, and the consequences of disobeying the rules.

Once when I was fishing with a friend on the creek nearest our home, we caught the biggest snapping turtle we'd ever seen. We wanted to show it to my parents, so we suspended it from a sapling and started home through the swamp and woods in the middle of the afternoon. We walked through a slow drizzle until after sundown, when we finally saw some tracks, which we were distressed to discover were our own! Realizing that we were lost, we dropped the turtle and concentrated on walking in a straight line. Then the skies cleared and we saw Venus, an evening star at the time, and walked westward by its guidance, in as straight a line as possible through the trees, vines, and swampy ground. I was thankful for my father's training about the more prominent heavenly bodies.

I had mixed emotions. The thing I wanted most was to see my daddy, but that was also what I feared most, realizing that we had violated all the woodsmen's techniques he had taught me. I also knew he would have mounted a search party when we did not return home.

We finally saw lights, which turned out to be in a farmer's cabin about ten miles from our house. Luckily, he had a mule and wagon, and volunteered to carry us home. Too exhausted to walk any farther, we accepted his offer. After traveling for a couple of miles, we met Daddy in his pickup.

We rode six miles over the dirt roads without speaking, my father obviously displeased. He turned to me when we arrived at home and said, "I thought you knew more about the woods than to get lost." Then he reached out to me, and I rushed to embrace him. I knew I deserved to be chastised, but just being in my father's arms was one of my most joyful and memorable experiences. For a few hours, without either of us knowing where the other was, there had been a vacuum in our lives.

COMING ALONGSIDE OUR KIDS

JOSH MCDOWELL

from *The Father Connection*

The 1992 Olympics in Barcelona featured one of the most memorable moments of sports history.

Derek Redmond of Great Britain was on the way to fulfilling a lifetime dream, that of winning a gold medal in the Olympics. He had earned a spot in the semifinals of the 400-meter race, and as the gun sounded to start the race, Derek got off to a great start. He was running the race of his life, and the finish line was in sight, when suddenly he felt a stab of pain in his right leg. He pitched face-first to the track with a torn hamstring. The race was over for Derek.

He struggled to his feet before the medical team could reach him. Though every runner had passed him, he began hopping forward, tears of pain and disappointment streaking his face, determined to finish the race. Suddenly, a man plowed through the security guards on the sidelines and ran onto the track.

He raced up to Derek and hugged him. "You don't have to do this," Jim Redmond told his weeping son.

"Yes, I do," Derek answered.

"Well, then," his father said, "we're going to finish this together."

Derek's father gripped his son around the shoulders, and they faced the finish line, resolutely waving off the security men who hovered about them. They limped and hopped together, Derek's head sometimes buried in his father's shoulder, and stayed in Derek's lane all the way to the end.

The watching crowd gaped at first at the unusual scene. Then, one by one, they rose to their feet, and began cheering and crying at the son's determination and the father's support.

How many times have I stayed in the stands when I should have run onto the track to support my kids? Too many, I must confess. But becoming a refuge to my children will mean running to their side, not to carry them, but to come alongside them when they face hurt and disappointment. It will mean saying, "We're going to finish this together." It will mean enduring the stares of the crowd and ignoring the cries of critics. It may be personally risky, it may be professionally unwise, but it will be worth it to hear my kids say, "Thanks, Dad, you're my defender."

———————

Editor's Note: *Maybe you've been there. Without warning, everything you've planned for and worked hard for—your entire life!—came crashing down at your feet. Maybe it was a disaster—a force of nature—that destroyed your physical home. Maybe it was a divorce that destroyed your family home. Maybe you were terminated from a job with undue notice and for no apparent reason. The race that you had prepared to run ended as abruptly as Derek Redmond's race, and it seemed the whole world passed you by. Your life lay in pieces, and the thought of quitting loomed before you as the only feasible alternative. Who could blame you?*

But, like Derek Redmond, you decided to finish the race. Why? You had no chance of winning. You had no chance of fulfilling the dream you had set out to accomplish. But, determinedly, you began to place one foot in front of the other. Suddenly, someone burst through the crowd and came alongside you. It was your heavenly Father.

"You don't have to do this," he says to you. And yet, you both know that you do. "Then we'll finish this together," he says, as he wraps his arm around your shoulder and limps forward with you to the finish line.

And as you hobble, side-by-side, the air is electrified as the audience is enthralled. Rising to their feet, a low rumble begins to form above the clapping of hands. Their applause—an inadequate expression of praise for such a meritorious event—is muffled by the stomping of their feet. The sound rises to a fever-high pitch as together the Father and son cross the finish line.

The Father, the son, the decision, the determination.

THE WORST GAME OF MY LIFE!

STEPHEN R. COVEY

from *Living the Seven Habits*

Experience in this story the power of focusing on effort and relationship rather than on expectations and results.

I was the junior varsity quarterback at the college I attended. The previous week, we had had a great game. I threw for about five hundred yards, four or five touchdowns, and the newspaper started heralding me as the next great quarterback.

The following week we got set to play one of the best teams in the nation. Their leading defensive lineman was a 275-pound quarterback-wrecking machine.

We were playing at home for this big game. Of course, I wanted to play well in front of the home crowd. And my dad flew back from somewhere just to watch me play. I didn't think he would make it, but there he was just before the whistle blew.

I had the worst game of my life. The monster defensive lineman was all over me. He spent more time in our backfield than I did. My head was slammed into the ground so many times I was leaving divots. I swear I wasn't on my feet after the snap for longer than three seconds. Of course, I didn't throw one touchdown. I did, however, rack up an impressive number of interceptions. We lost by about thirty points.

During the game I must have looked pathetic. After the game I was embarrassed. Nobody would talk to me. You know how it goes when you play terribly? In the locker room, everybody avoids you. So I showered and dressed in silence. When I came out of the locker room, my dad was waiting for me. He took me in his arms, hugged me, looked me right in the eyes and said, "That's the best game I have ever seen you play. Not because you won or threw the most touchdowns. But because I have never seen you be as tough as you had to be out there today. You were getting beat. Yet you kept getting up. I have never been so proud of you." And he meant it.

I felt so good. Good because my dad was proud of me, but also good because what he said affirmed what I had been feeling. In the back of my mind, despite the bruises and the jarring, I had been thinking, "I'm hanging in here. I'm getting back up. I'm playing tough today." My dad was the only person who recognized that in me. For him to tell me that changed my whole perspective on that dreadful game. It was a moment I will never forget and was a great bonding experience for me and my dad.

Psychological confirmation takes place when you agree with what the other person is feeling inside. This young man was feeling that he was tough and hanging in there, even though the results were disastrous. When the father confirmed the boy's psychological state, the boy felt understood and appreciated [Habit 5: Seek First to Understand, Then to Be Understood]. The father was not concerned with social expectations, but with the relationship and the intrinsic value of effort.

I had a similar experience on my son Sean's twenty-second birthday. He had given his all as the starting quarterback during the first half of a major university football game, but it wasn't working and he was pulled in the second half. I had given him an engraved plaque earlier that day for his birthday because I had a premonition something like this might happen. He said it was one of the greatest presents he had received in his life. It was a quote that captures the spirit of the Olympic Creed and reads as follows: "Ask not yourself for victory, but for courage, for if you endure, you bring honor to yourself; and even more, you bring honor to us all."

A TIME TO BE BORN

PHILIP GULLEY

from *For Everything a Season*

I was born deep in the winter. Each birthday my father phones to recount the events surrounding my birth. Our sons are asleep in their bedroom under the eaves. My wife and I are sitting in front of the fireplace; she is doing her needlework and I am reading a mystery. The phone rings. I ease out of my chair, walk to the kitchen, pick up the phone and say "Hello."

It is my father. No "Hello." No "How are you?" Just the same question each birthday: "Have I ever told you what happened the night you were born?"

"I don't believe so," I tell him.

"Well, it was eight o'clock in the evening when your mother went into labor. I remember the time because *Gunsmoke* was just starting. There was a terrible snowstorm. We could barely see the neighbor's house for the snow. We got in the car to drive to the hospital in the city. Our defroster didn't work, and I couldn't see through the windshield. I had to drive the whole twenty miles with my head out the window. It was so cold my face was frostbitten. I ran a red light and a policeman pulled me over and said he was going to give me a ticket. I told him to hurry up because my wife was going to have a baby. The policeman said, 'Follow me!' and he turned on his lights and siren and off we went, all the way to the hospital where you were born. You had a police escort to the hospital. Not everyone can say that. That makes you special."

When I was a child, my mother would tuck me into bed, kiss my forehead, then leave the room. My father would come in and sit at the foot of my bed and ask, "Say, have I ever told you what happened the night you were born?"

"I don't believe so," I would tell him.

He would lean back, close his eyes, and conjure up that memory— the snow and the swirling red lights and the siren's wail. I've heard that story nearly forty times and I never tire of it. Every year I wonder the same things: Will they make it in time? Will I be all right? Of course I will be, because here I am. But the way my father tells the story leaves the outcome in doubt and I never quite relax until the story concludes with me safely delivered.

In my teenage years, when my father and I were at odds, I would remember how he suffered frostbite to bring me safely into this world . . . and my heart would soften. I was a skinny child, the target of bullies. When beaten up and ridiculed, I would take comfort in the fact that I was ushered into this world with a police escort and they were not. It was a wonderful gift my father gave me, that story. He could not give me wealth or fame to ease my way so he gave me that story and it provided a deep consolation.

My chief regret is that I am not able to offer my sons a similar story. Their births were routine, insofar as a child's birth is ever routine. We had sufficient time to drive to the hospital. The roads were clear. The car ran smoothly. My wife was unruffled. The doctors and nurses were competent and our children were delivered with a minimum of pain. I didn't feel a thing.

When my older son turned five years old, he asked me, "Daddy, what happened when I was born?" I didn't want to tell him the truth—that as births go, his was unremarkable, with only one peculiarity. When he was due to emerge, I was in the hospital rest room reading a back issue of *Reader's Digest.* Drama in Real Life. A man ran off the road and over a cliff, where he lay broken and dazed for three days before spelling out *HELP* with rocks and sticks. Spotted by an airplane, he was rescued and lived to share his dramatic story.

As I finished reading his harrowing tale, the nurse knocked on the door and said, "Your wife is having your baby. You better get out here." So I came out and five minutes later, so did my son. That is the truth, though it isn't the kind of story I want to tell my son. It is not the stuff of legend. So when he asked me what happened when he was born, I kissed his forehead and took my place at the foot of his bed.

"Yours was a very special birth," I told him. "Quite miraculous. It was the middle of winter. It was snowing. We were sitting in the living room late in the evening. Your mother went into labor. We climbed into the car and made our way toward the hospital. The roads were terribly slick. As we were rounding a curve, we slid off the road and over a cliff, where our car came to rest at the bottom. We were dazed and bruised. Your mother was pinned in the wreckage and couldn't move, but I could, just barely. I managed to climb through a window and gather some sticks and rocks, which I used to spell out *HELP*. The next morning, an airplane, circling overhead, spotted us and we were rescued. We were rushed to a hospital where you were safely delivered. And that, son, is the story of your birth."

He swelled with pride. He'd had no idea his beginnings were marked with such drama. "Tell me again," he pleaded.

"Next year," I told him. "You'll have to wait until your next birthday." I kissed him good night and went downstairs to sit in my chair. My wife was there.

"What were you and Spencer talking about?" Joan asked.

"I was telling him about the night he was born," I answered.

"Did you mention how the nurse had to get you out of the restroom because you were reading that story in *Reader's Digest*?"

"Indirectly," I answered.

"I hope you haven't put ideas in his head," she said.

My wife is a straightforward woman who doesn't always appreciate the advantage of story and drama. She doesn't need to embellish her birth story. Her mother delivered her without assistance after the doctor had left for the day. With a birth like that, you don't need to exaggerate. It's miracle enough.

I went back upstairs to talk with Spencer. "I would prefer," I told him, "that you not talk with your mother about the car wreck and your birth. The memory of it is more than she can bear."

My birthday came a few weeks later. My parents invited us for Sunday dinner. We were seated in the dining room. I said to my father, "Tell me about my birth, about the policeman and the snow."

"What policeman?" my mother asked. "What snow?"

"The policeman who escorted you and Dad to the hospital the night I was born. Remember? It was snowing and the defroster was broken and Dad got frostbite from driving twenty miles with his head out the window."

Mom said, "It wasn't snowing—it was unusually warm that day. And he wouldn't take me to the hospital until *Gunsmoke* was over. It was his favorite show, you know. He almost named you Festus."

I looked across the table at my father. He smiled, winked, and said nothing. It was all a story—no snow, no policeman, no frostbite, no siren, no swirling lights. But it was my story, true or not, and I was grateful for it. I did not have wealth or fame or muscles or good looks to ease my way into this world. But I did have my story. My father gave it to me. It was his gift to me, bestowed with love, and I treasure it.

Later that night I was sitting in our living room. The phone rang. It was my father. "Say, have I ever told you what happened the night you were born?" he asked.

"I don't believe so," I answered.

He spoke of blowing snow and running a red light and how he got frostbite. He told about the policeman who pulled him over and the police escort with the swirling lights and the siren.

"Not everyone gets a police escort," he pointed out. "That makes you special."

These are the stories passed from father to son. We have no wealth to bestow, no fame to offer. We have only these legends to remind our children that on the day they were born, the ordinary was suspended and the miracles flew thick.

THE SUNSET

ELSA KOK CINJÉE

I was only twelve, an age when I loved and hated with the same level of intensity. My relationship with my father was good, but I was entering into those years when I wanted to separate myself, to grow up. I wanted to live! I was the youngest, and I had four older brothers. They were all out of the home, and on this particular family vacation, it was just my parents and I. Wherever we stopped, I quickly made friends with other children. We met, we played, and we said our good-byes. It was the way of summer.

One of our stops brought us to a deserted inlet on the coast of Long Island. We spent the morning searching for clams and the afternoon catching spider crabs from the dusky water. As the sun began to set, I took a walk with my father. It was one of those rare moments of quiet. There was no one else walking along the beach; the only sound was that of the crashing waves. The colors playing out before us included an amazing combination of reds, pinks, purples, and yellows.

My father and I walked side by side, the beauty before us binding our hearts together. He draped his arm around my shoulders, and I nestled mine around his waist. My heart felt full. I can still bring that memory into the forefront of my mind and almost taste the salt water in the air. I remember looking up at my father's face and feeling this magical intensity to my love for him. He was my dad! He was wonderful! I can still recall how he pointed to the feather-like dusting of the clouds and how they seemed to direct our gaze to the setting sun. His face, bathed in that light, was as beautiful as the scene playing out before us. In that moment it felt like a piece of heaven to be nestled under his arm. I felt more love for my dad than I could contain.

Now, years later, any time the sun sets and the darkness rolls in to bring closure to the day, I find myself transported back to that moment of perfection on a deserted Long Island seashore. I am reminded of my dad, but also of my heavenly Father. For it was my heavenly Father that created the beauty my dad and I shared. In that one moment, I knew the best of both fathers. And the feeling lasts.

The way my dad showed his love for me that evening gave me a glimpse of our Father's love. The comfort and tenderness I felt in my dad's arms is akin to the feeling I have when I am connected to my Savior. Now with each sunset, I can imagine God walking beside me, a smile on his face as he points out the beauty of his creation. I can envision what he might look like, with the final rays of light dancing across his features. For this I remain grateful to both fathers, who, when I was twelve years old, gave me a simple gift I'll never forget.

FEAR NO EVIL...
EXCEPT

CORRIE TEN BOOM

from *In My Father's House*

A child is not fearless, contrary to what his parents may think at times. A child is often a bundle of unexpressed fears, unknown terrors, and shadowy worries. I was afraid of the doctor's office, my family's leaving me, and the mystery of death.

Nollie's nightgown was my contact with security. We slept in the same bed, and I can remember clinging to Nollie's nightgown as long as she would allow me. Poor Nollie, when she would try to turn, she would be anchored by my little fist clasping her tightly.

One time Mother took Nollie and me to visit a woman whose baby had died. I wished Nollie had been allowed to wear her nightgown on that journey, because I needed desperately to hang onto it.

We climbed a narrow staircase and entered the poorly furnished room of one of Mama's "lame ducks" (the name we children had given to her protégées). Although we often did not have sufficient money for ourselves, Mother always found someone who was in greater need.

In that shabby little room was a crib with a baby inside. It didn't move at all and its skin was very white. Nollie stood next to the crib and touched the baby's cheek.

"Feel that," she said to me, "it's so cold."

I touched the little hand, and then ran to my mother and buried my face in her lap. I had touched death for the first time, and it seemed that the impression of cold remained with me for hours and hours.

When we returned home, I ran up the narrow stairs to my bedroom and leaned against the antique chest of drawers. There was an enormous fear in my heart—almost terror. In my imagination, I pictured the future in which I saw myself all alone, my family gone, and myself left desolate. My family was my security, but that day I saw death, and knew that they could die, too. I had never thought about it before.

The dinner bell rang downstairs, and I was so grateful to go to the big oval table, and get warm again, and feel the security of being with my family. I thought how stupid the grown-ups would think I was if I told them about the fear that was still in my heart.

I ate dinner quietly that night, which was not easy when you are in the midst of such a lively family. Our dinner table spilled over with conversation.

After dinner Father took the Bible, as he always did, and began to read the lines from Psalms 46:2. "Therefore will not we fear, though the earth be removed, and though the mountains be carried into the midst of the sea" (KJV).

I sat up straight in my chair and stared at my father. I didn't know much about mountains, living in flat, flat Holland, but I certainly knew a lot about fear. I thought Papa must have known exactly what my problem was that night.

My faith in Papa, and in the words he read from the Bible, was absolute. If they said not to fear, then God would take care of it. I felt secure again.

SECTION *Nine*

The FELLOWSHIP OF A FATHER

MY FATHER'S HANDS
TERESA CLEARY

The hands that lie on top of the smooth, white hospital bed sheet are liver-spotted and swollen. The nails are brittle and tinged with yellow. My father's body is shutting down—preparing to die—but I am not ready.

I cradle one of those hands in my own and realize it's turning cold. These hands are so familiar and yet so strange. They are not the hands I remember . . .

The feel of my father's hands firmly on my back as a child, the swing flying higher and higher in the air, are the ones I remember. "Harder, Daddy! Push harder!" I called. With mighty strength and great gentleness, he complied.

As a teenager I remember the firm clasp of my father's hand as he greeted me after high school honors night. "I'm so proud of you!" he announced as he shook my hand before pulling me into his arms for a hug. After years of hard work, those were the words I longed to hear.

As a young woman I remember my dad's hand covering mine as I took his arm before he walked me down the aisle to join my husband-to-be. "You're beautiful," he said with a squeeze of his hand. In his eyes, I always was.

A few short years later I remember those hands as they first held my son, Micah Charles Cleary. Micah's middle name was in honor of my father. I wanted both the newest and the oldest man in my life to know, in this small way, how much they were loved.

As a child, it seemed it was only the firm grasp of my father's hand that kept me safe. Whether holding me after a nightmare, bandaging a skinned knee, or explaining a difficult math problem, those hands calmed my fears, eased my pain, and showed me the way.

As an adult, my father's guidance was evident as I struggled with a choice of career.

"What should I do?" I asked him after deciding that yet another college major wasn't for me.

"What do you love?" he replied. "Decide what that is and turn it into a career. After all, you'll be doing it for a lifetime."

From those wise words, a writing career was born.

My father's guidance was always straight and sure—just like the guidance I receive from my heavenly Father through reading his Word and going before him in prayer.

It is so easy to see the hand of God in my relationship with my earthly father. Because of my dad I can relate to God as One who desires to be personally involved in my life. Day after day, in ways that were simple and yet profound, I saw divine love expressed through the touch of my father's hands in my life.

And yet now it was time to let go of those hands that I'd held so dear.

"I love you, Dad," I whispered one final time. "Go, and be with Jesus."

With a ragged sigh, my father breathed his last. I held on for a moment not wanting to give up. Not wanting to let go. Yet as I released his hand, I knew Another had already taken it. I knew my father was walking hand in hand with Jesus as he was welcomed into Paradise.

PRESENTS AND PRESENCE

Presents and Presence

PHILIP GULLEY

from *Front Porch Tales*

When Joan and I were expecting our first child, we received the usual warnings regarding lack of sleep, dirty diapers, and temper tantrums. Still, we looked forward to being parents. That's because no one told us about birthday parties.

When our oldest son neared age three, we mistakenly asked him what he wanted for his birthday. At first, all he wanted was a tricycle. We thought that was cute, so we made a big deal out of it. Thus encouraged, he asked for the entire toy department at Wal-Mart. A friend of ours with four kids laughed when we told her about this. She said our first mistake was telling him he had a birthday.

One of my friends has a daughter a few months older than our son, which is the worst possible thing that could have happened because they give great parties for their child, which gets ours pumped up for his. When their daughter turned three, they actually rented a pony for her birthday party. The rest of us were livid, because now we would have to hire a pony for our kids. Thank God, the pony went nuts and bucked a kid off, so my son doesn't want anything to do with ponies. I guess it's true that all things work together for good for those who love the Lord.

Then there's always the little matter of whom to invite to your children's birthday parties. We invite a lot of people, for two reasons. First, the more stuff our kids get from other people, the less we have to buy. Second, a lot of people have made us mad, and this is a good way to pay them back. Like our "friend" who faked a Mexican accent and said, "Sorry, no speaka English," when we were calling around looking for a babysitter.

I know a guy who's a Jehovah's Witness. They don't celebrate birthday parties. When I asked him why, he said it's because the only birthday party in the Bible cost John the Baptist his head. And here I am moaning that my son's birthday cost me an arm and a leg.

One birthday our oldest boy got so many toys he sat in the living room and cried. All those options overwhelmed him. I know how he felt. I feel that way whenever *The Andy Griffith Show* and *Murder, She Wrote* are on at the same time.

When I was growing up, I never had a big birthday party. There were five children in my family, and Mom and Dad couldn't afford the extravagance. Mom tried to make things special by letting the birthday child decide what we'd have for dinner. We thought that was a treat! Now my wife and I are so tired of deciding what to have for supper, we'd eat monkey tongues if someone showed up to cook them.

You probably won't like my saying this, but I've noticed a correlation between the size of birthday parties and parental employment. If both parents work, a kid can pretty well count on having a big party. I think parents do that to make up for being gone so much. Call me crazy, but I believe children need our presence more than they need our presents.

I've forgotten almost every present my parents ever gave me. But I'll never forget that when I turned twelve my dad took me canoeing for an entire day. So there are presents and there is presence. Blessed are those parents who learn the finer gift early on.

THE ROCK OF GIBRALTAR

GAIL E. B. PADILLA

It never seemed strange to me. I didn't know I was the only child in the neighborhood who had a "weekend dad." I assumed that all dads picked up their children every Friday night.

From my granite perch at the end of our gravel driveway, I would sit every Friday night as I watched the cars on the main highway whiz by. From my earliest memory until my preteen years, I played the game. I counted the cars and wondered how many automobiles would pass before Dad's blue car would turn toward me. One, two, three . . . ninety-nine, one hundred? I always guessed wrong. More cars passed by than I wanted before Dad's vehicle appeared. I knew approximately when Dad would arrive, because we synchronized our watches before he left his house, and I knew how long it took, provided there were no unforeseen circumstances to hold him up.

On hot, humid nights, I wanted a drink of cold Kool-Aid, but I thought I might miss the thrill of seeing Dad's Plymouth in the distance if I went into the house to get it. The temptation to "wet my whistle," as Dad used to say, was pretty strong at times. Nevertheless, I continued to wait with great anticipation. *He'll be car number 450, or 800*, I'd guess.

During inclement weather, I stood guard at the picture window in the living room. Only drenched leaves or barren branches met my gaze, but I still counted. *One thousand one, one thousand two, one thousand three . . .* The seconds turned into minutes, and sometimes I waited for what seemed a really long time. But I always thought it was well worth it.

The rural outdoor setting where I lived brought me great joy. I felt close to God when outside, partly because of the drastic seasonal changes.

Minnows in our creek teased my fingers as I tried to catch them. The Tuscarawas River offered raft-building opportunities. Everywhere I played, open areas of sky cover seemed to protect me.

But none of the natural beauty overcame my desire to escape on weekends, because inside the house, where I lived with my mother and stepfather, it was a different world. It was dark, abusive, vise-like. I felt I needed the two-day respite every week, which contributed to my intense anticipation on Friday nights. My dad would take me to stay with him and my grandmother. I looked forward to the quietness of their home. Grandma had a secret banana cake recipe that she usually baked before I raced up the back steps into her arms. She slathered it with what she called Depression icing. It was delicious. I remember she covered the cake with a tea towel to keep it fresh.

Grandma nourished me well so Dad could take me on "adventures." He had served in the Civilian Conservation Corps during his youth. I thought then, and now, that he knew everything about survival in our country's habitat. Dad taught me as much as my young mind would allow. From him I learned to navigate a waterway of lakes in a canoe. I found it easy to recognize our surroundings by nature's landmarks.

Saturday nights, I would always say, "Dad, let's drive up Cherry Street hill." I was the Krispy Kreme fan and expert.

Like clockwork, he would respond, "All righty. I'll order the donuts."

Dad picked up the receiver on his black rotary-dial telephone. From memory he dialed the number. "What time will you pull a new batch of donuts from the oven?" he always asked.

After he relayed the information to me, we waited in front of a board game: Monopoly or Sorry. Although I concentrated on winning, I did not forget our mission. Dad's answer to my impatience was always the same: "It's five minutes past the last time you asked."

When the proper moment arrived, Dad and I walked to the rented garage where he parked his car. He always wrapped his strong, sturdy, calloused fingers around my small hand.

Along the way, he'd sometimes talk to me about car maintenance. I learned how often the oil should be changed. I knew about windshield wiper replacement. And he said, "One of these days, I'm going to teach you how to change a tire." He didn't think anyone should get a driver's license until she could change a flat tire.

I listened in silence, because I didn't really care at the time about how to take care of a car. What I did care about was the thrill I felt when Dad drove me up and down "the steepest hill in town."

As Dad's car approached Cherry Street, he would always tease me: Did I think I was too small to conquer such a mountain? By myself, I would be scared. But with Dad at the steering wheel, I knew we'd make it just fine. Sometimes it felt like my stomach was in my throat, and I would holler, "Help, Daddy! I can't see the top of the hill. We'll never make it; we're going to roll backwards."

My disquiet made Dad laugh, and he would reach out his hand and steady me with his protective love. I took the cue and quit hollering.

When we reached the summit, I clapped with delighted relief. "That's better than any roller coaster," I said.

The donuts on the other side of the hill were really for Dad. Cherry Street was for me. It gave me the weekly release I needed.

I don't think Dad ever realized that I considered our time together my lifeline to sanity. But he never let me down. After work he would eat a quick dinner with Grandma, then shower before heading out from the city to pick up his only child in farm-country.

Now that my dad is gone, I regret that I failed to tell him how much I appreciated his dependability. The perfect opportunity came when I picked him up at the nursing home during the last spring of his eighty-three years. I took him to the Cincinnati Nature Center, where I pushed his wheelchair along the asphalt hiking trail. I did not express my appreciation, but his comments told me that he remembered how his "little girl" used to pull open his car door with a squeal.

"Daddy, you're here! Let's go get a hamburger and a milkshake."

Dad had introduced me to those delicious hamburgers, grilled over a hot flame in a little hole-in-the-wall restaurant. I loved to watch the cook flip those burgers right before our eyes. Then he would put two scoops of ice cream, milk, and vanilla flavoring into a tall metal container and churn it until I could almost taste it. At just the right moment of perfection, he would pour the shake into a glass and then set it in front of me, adding the half-filled metal shaker at the side. "Pour yourself the rest when you're ready," he'd say.

In those days I didn't comprehend Dad's end-of-the-week fatigue or monetary sacrifice. I had to become a parent before I understood the surrender of a weekend. During my childhood, all I knew was that my dad loved me enough to show up without fail. Even in blizzard conditions.

During my youth, northern Ohio usually received its first serious snow by Thanksgiving and did not show grass again until spring. Yet my dad never canceled his visits with me. If a thick cloud of fluffy flakes obscured my view of the road from inside the house, I still waited. Whether I cooled my heels in fresh air or stale, I became antsy while I counted the cars. But my impatience never gave way to doubt. My dad *would* come. I knew that he loved me enough to show up as he had promised. The crunch of his tires against the deep snow would announce his arrival.

Life is full of problems that require a daddy's assistance. Often, only our heavenly Father can meet the challenge. We may pray once, twice, or more than a hundred times for his help. As his children, we become impatient with God. We may think that he is never going to liberate us.

I have heard people say that our heavenly Father is a "last-minute God." Sometimes it seems that he waits until the last possible moment to meet our crises.

Although my dad had a talent for understanding the environment, he could not do everything. God is capable of doing the impossible. He may choose to do it in a manner we hadn't thought of, or in a time frame other than our own. I learned from waiting for my human father that we can't always understand the delays encountered along the way, because we do not have complete information. The observations we make do not show us what God endures or who else he is protecting. Nevertheless, God is the Rock worthy of resting on as we wait for a reprieve from our captivities or storms of life.

Our heavenly Father understands our edginess—our need to conquer the Cherry Street hills of life in order to find relief from our difficulties. When God drives with us to the summit, he sees and feels *all* the challenges we face. Nothing is hidden from his view. Like my dad, God understands that there are conditions when deliberate, steady driving is in our best interest. My dad used to tell me that he had to slow down in bad weather in order to keep everyone safe. He wanted to get to me, but he had to protect the other drivers too. God also considers other people, but he can plow through the steepest incline in order to rescue us.

When my dad explained his snowy night tardiness, he would say, "Better late than never."

God's assurance guarantees more comfort, because he will never slide off an ice-covered road into a ditch. We have his promise, "I will never leave you nor forsake you."

LESSONS ON ICE

PHIL CALLAWAY

from *Who Put the Skunk in the Trunk?*

The juggler comes closest to our hearts when he misses the ball.
—Richard J. Needham

Ever since I was knee-high to a referee, I've been crazy about sports. I grew up in Canada where the national religion is ice hockey; where children and adults alike attend weekly (and sometimes daily) services at their local arena and never complain about the length of the sermon. Each winter morning I could be found strapping on ice skates, tripping down the road making sparks fly all the way to the outdoor rink. There, from the time I was three years old, I learned to play hockey with the big boys. I learned to stickhandle with the best of them. To fire the puck with utmost accuracy. I also mastered the art of gliding effortlessly across a frozen sheet of ice, sometimes on my back, often crashing headfirst into the boards and waking up the following Wednesday, wearing a bewildered expression.

Maybe it's the result of getting hit with a puck one too many times, but I miss those days.

Back then Saturday night was bath night. We would file into the tub from the eldest to the youngest to scrub a week's worth of play from our bodies. This was one of those times when it didn't pay off to be the youngest of five. By the time it was my turn the water was rather murky, to say the least, and so I couldn't wait to get to the living room and gather around the Philco radio for hockey night in Canada. Ah, how I loved the roar of the crowd. The tension of overtime. Players' names that brought visions of grandeur: Gordie Howe, Frank Mahovilich, Bobby Orr, Phil Callaway. It's true, I imagined the announcer, his voice rushed with excitement: "It's Callaway, blazing down the ice . . . splitting the defense . . . he shoots . . . he scores! Oh my, I have not seen anything this exciting since the Allies invaded Normandy!"

Certain that this was my calling, I pursued my dream with everything I had.

Before long I was playing with real teams in real arenas with real helmets to protect our really hard heads. Each Saturday morning we took to the ice in an empty building while the rest of the world slept. Occasionally I would look up into the bleachers to discover that today they weren't quite so empty. That Dad was there. Somehow after a long week, he had summoned the energy to haul himself out of bed just to watch me play. Dad seemed to think I displayed more talent than the Toronto Maple Leafs and the New York Rangers combined, and he would tell the world this, hollering loudly when I scored (twice that year) and clapping his big leather gloves together.

I wanted desperately to hear those gloves smack, and I couldn't wait to play professionally. I would fly Mom and Dad to the games. Buy them front row seats right behind the players. They could help the coach make important decisions.

We won only one game that year (the other team's goalie didn't show up), but Dad always encouraged me.

"Son," he would say as we walked home from the rink, Dad lugging my heavy equipment, me carrying my hockey stick, "you're not the first one to walk into a brick wall." Then he would recount historical failures: Thomas Edison struck out in his first two thousand attempts to invent the light bulb; Henry Ford went broke five times before finally succeeding in creating a car.

"But, Dad," I said, "our Ford Meteor won't start. That's why we're walking."

"Son," he'd answer, undaunted, "never mind about that. You just be like a postage stamp. You stick to it till you get there."

In tenth grade, we stuck to it, posting our first winning season and earning the adulation of a few hundred teenage girls. It was a milestone year for me. In fact, something occurred that changed my dreams for good.

It happened like this.

Late March. The championship game. An event of such magnitude in our small town that a crowd of millions, or at least a few hundred, packed our small arena to watch the stars come out. Peering in nervous anticipation through a crack in the locker room door, I had the distinct feeling that this would be my night. The years of stickhandling were about to pay off. Those who had paid the scalpers twenty-five cents would not be disappointed.

But as the game progressed, my dream began to fade. In fact, as the clock ran down to the final minute, the dream had all the makings of a nightmare. We were behind 3–2 as I climbed over the boards. The final buzzer was about to sound. The fat lady was about to sing. We needed a miracle. We needed Phil Callaway.

And so I took a pass from the corner and skillfully rifled the puck past a sprawling goalie. The red goal light came on. The girls went wild. The game was tied. And I was a hero. I had scored the goal of my dreams.

Only one goal could top it. The overtime goal.

As I sat in the dressing room waiting for the ice to be cleared I eased open the locker room door for a peek at the crowd. Prepare yourselves, you lucky people. Tonight destiny is on my side. Tonight will be *my* night. You will remember me for years to come. Last week when I missed the open net, you chanted my name reassuringly:

> That's all right, that's okay.
> We still love you Callaway.

But not tonight. No need for sympathy, thank you. Only applause. Wild, exuberant, adoring applause.

And, sure enough, about five minutes into overtime I scored the winning goal. It is a moment that is forever available to me on instant replay and sometimes in slow motion. As the puck slid toward the open net, I dove, trying desperately to forge its direction. As the crowd rose to its feet, I swatted the puck across the goal line.

The red light lit.

The girls screamed.

But they were not cheering for me.

I had just scored into my own net.

I don't remember much that happened after that. In fact, the next number of years are a bit of a blur. I do remember making a beeline for the locker room where I sat down and threw a white towel over my head. And I recall the comments of my fellow teammates: "Don't worry about it, Callaway. Anyone coulda done that . . . if he was totally uncoordinated."

I pulled the towel around my ears to muffle the laughter. Then I unlaced my skates. And hung them up. For good.

I couldn't have known that NBA legend Michael Jordan would be cut from his high school basketball team, that Louis L'Amour's first western was rejected 350 times by publishers, or that Albert Einstein had trouble with simple math equations (his wife helped him fill out his tax returns). It might have helped me to know that a dozen years earlier the manager of the Grand Ole Opry fired an up-and-coming singer after only one performance, advising him to go back to driving a truck. Elvis Presley pursued a singing career anyway. But I wasn't thinking of Elvis on this night.

Instead, I left the building. All shook up.

Upon arriving home, I headed straight for my room. A bad case of the flu had kept Dad from the game.

"How did it go?" he asked, standing in my doorway, studying my pale face and knowing part of the answer.

"Aw, Dad," I said, hanging my head. "I can't tell you. You're sick enough."

Flopping onto my bed, I put my hands behind my head and stared at the stucco ceiling. Dad entered my room and sat beside me, saying nothing.

"Did you ever do something so stupid you wished for all the world you could go back twenty-four hours and start the day again?" I asked.

"Well," said Dad, "there was the time I shot out Old Man Henderson's headlights with my .22 . . . and then there was—"

I interrupted him for the first time in years. Then sat up. Buried my head in my fists. And told him everything: The shock of the crowd. The shame of the dressing room. My play that would live in infamy. I didn't dare look at his face. The face of a proud dad. A dad who had some big dreams of his own for his youngest son.

There was silence for a minute. Then Dad put his hand on my knee and did the most unexpected thing in the world.

He began to laugh.

And I couldn't believe I was doing it . . . but I joined him.

It was the last thing either of us expected. It was the very best thing.

More than twenty years have passed since the night Dad and I sat on the edge of my bed laughing together. I remember it as the night I determined to skate again. In fact, I'm still skating. I've even managed to score a few goals over the years. Into the right net. But no goal will ever be as memorable as that overtime goal. A lifelong reminder that life's biggest victories can be found in the ruins of defeat.

For several years after that I'd wake up in a cold sweat reliving that overtime goal, but when I'd remember Dad's hand on my knee . . . I'd smile from ear to ear. You see, that was the night I discovered something that has made the heaviest burdens seem a whole lot lighter.

It is the simple fact that no matter what I've done, no matter where I've been, no matter how bad my world seems, my Father loves me. Isaiah said it best when he wrote:

> " 'For the mountains may depart and the hills disappear,
> but even then I will remain loyal to you . . .' says the Lord, who has
> mercy on you." (Isaiah 54:10)

Dad may not have known it, but that night he gave me a priceless glimpse into the face of my heavenly Father.

A face full of compassion, forgiveness, and grace.

A smiling face.

The face of One who laughs.

IN HIS PRESENCE

VICKIE JENKINS

My screams could be heard all over the floor. Tears rolled down my face. I had been born with very bad eyes, and now, as a preschooler, I was on my way to the operating room at Children's Hospital. I was struggling for all I was worth as I peered around the doctors from the gurney they were rolling me on down the long hallway to surgery. I remember their green scrubs and white surgical masks. They had told my parents this third operation would make a drastic improvement in my eyesight.

I continued to cry, stretching my arms toward my parents, who stood at the end of the hallway behind a small glass window.

"Daddy, Mommy, I don't wanna go! I don't wanna go! Mommy! Daddy!"

They wheeled me through the large swinging doors, and that is the last thing I remember before surgery.

When I woke up, my eyes hurt. Patches of gauze coverd my eyes, and the darkness scared me. I called again for my parents.

"Mommy! Daddy! Where are you?"

I wanted the comfort of knowing that they were there beside me. Then I heard their consoling voices—the gentle, soothing tone of my mother, and the strong voice of my father.

"Everything is going to be okay," my dad said as his strong arms wrapped around me in a gentle hug.

I was in a crib-like bed with the sidebar halfway down. My parents stood with their arms draped over the railing.

"Here's a special gift for my special little girl," my father said, placing a stuffed animal at my side. I smiled.

"Feel how soft it is," he said, as he took my hand and stroked my fingers across it. My father held my tiny hand within his. I squeezed his fingers as tight as I could, never wanting to let go. I felt safe and secure, and then I fell asleep.

Through God's miraculous ways, that was the last eye surgery I needed. My stay at the hospital remains a gentle reminder of my childhood. The fact that my parents never left my side, staying with me night and day, would always be planted in my heart.

My father was a kind man. His kindness was magnified as he showered others with it as they crossed his path. He was everyone's friend. My mother was compassionate, and my father was giving and strong in character. Oh, how I loved my mother and father!

I find myself recapturing special memories that are tucked away in my heart. I can visualize the long hallway of the hospital, leading to the operating room. I can hear my own cries, but I can also hear the comforting words of my parents as they stood beside me, giving me the most precious gift they could give: themselves.

The sunlight is coming through the window. Like a spotlight, its beams center on a small stuffed animal. It's the little red monkey that was placed at my side so many years ago. Its head is tilted to the side; the rounded ears are lopsided. The faded yellow ribbon around its neck is frayed and worn. But it holds memories of my childhood trauma contrasted with my father's gentle hand on mine, and his warm smile.

As time moved on our lives changed, but the love continued. My mother, at seventy-four years of age, was dying of cancer and had been bedridden for two years. During her entire ordeal, my father took care of her.

Now my father and I stood at her bedside, embracing each other with tears and consolation. It seemed as though every moment I had ever shared with my mother began to unfold before me. The gentleness and sweetness were still evident in her face. My father's face showed signs of weariness. He leaned over the bed and gently kissed my mother, then lifted her limp hand and held it firmly.

"I'm here for you, and I'm not going to leave you." Tears ran down his cheeks as he prayed that God's will be done and that he would give her peace. That night my mother went to be with the Lord.

Two years later I still visit my father often and we share some happy moments together. The closeness my mother and I once knew has transferred to my father and me. We are closer than ever.

Even though I am a grown woman, sometimes I feel as though I am a child again, afraid of the unknown, confused, and alone. I want to cry out, "God, where are you?"

But I know God is there for me and that he has never left me. I hear my father's comforting words to my mother on her deathbed: "I'm here for you. I will never leave you." And I know God says those same words to me.

IN MY FATHER'S HOUSE

CAROL JACKSON

As I got back into my police car the dispatcher's voice boomed over the radio. "Cars 24 and 25, respond to 7234 Bendwell.* Disturbance. Man with a gun. Caller says his daughter's boyfriend is outside their residence creating a commotion, acting crazy, waving a handgun. Suspect is believed to be on drugs."

Calls of civil unrest are common on the police force. After fifteen years as a police officer, this call sounded no different to me than hundreds I'd heard before. It didn't take long, however, to discover that this situation would be far from routine.

Officer Detrin, assigned to Car 25, arrived at the scene at the same time I did in Car 24. As I pulled up to the curb, an elderly gentleman came out to meet us.

"Thank God, you're here," he said. "He's acting real crazy, threatening to kill us. I want him arrested and off my property before he hurts someone. His name is Wilson. He's my daughter's boyfriend. He showed up here all bent out of shape, and told my daughter, Monica, he had smoked a joint laced with PCP."

My partner and I turned our attention toward the younger man, who was still shouting and waving a gun in the air.

"Monica, get out here! You can't hide from me and I ain't scared of your old man. I'll kill him if you don't come out," he shouted. "Old Man, you better get in the house where you belong. This don't concern you."

With our weapons drawn, we approached cautiously.

Wilson was about five foot six and had a muscular, stocky build. His

---

*Based on a true story. The address and names have been changed and some of the dialogue has been modified to protect the identities of those involved.

unfocused eyes and wild gestures fit a pattern. He definitely acted like a man on drugs, and as I stepped closer, I sensed he might lose control and start shooting.

"Wilson, drop your gun *now*. Drop it and step back. We don't want to have to hurt you," I said.

"You think I'm afraid of the big tough cops? I can blow you both away right now. Come on, shoot me if you're so tough. Come on. Look at you. You don't have the guts." Wilson laughed hysterically, still waving his gun around.

"Wilson, drop the gun now before we shoot. We're not playing games," I said as we inched closer to him. As we approached, Wilson hesitated and lowered the gun to his side.

"Y'all ain't playin'," he said. "All right. It don't have to be like that. Give me a minute. I'll drop the gun. But if I do, y'all better not shoot me 'cause I know how trigger happy y'all are."

Wilson dropped the gun and stepped back.

"Okay, it's dropped. Now what?"

As soon as the gun hit the ground, Detrin and I ran up and grabbed Wilson from both sides. He offered no resistance, and everything seemed to be under control. I followed Detrin to the police station to assist during the booking procedures.

At times I've wondered how a girl who grew up in a warm community in the Midwest ended up in a police uniform, arresting people and keeping the peace. I think I owe it all to my father. Living in my father's house, I always felt safe and protected. We lived in a spacious home. My bedroom was my favorite, partly because it was next to my father's bedroom. The world outside our home may have been filled with crime, trouble, and turmoil, but I always felt guarded by my dad. Because my dad always protected me, I chose to serve as a protector of others.

Outside the police station, Detrin had Wilson by the arm. Although he didn't cuff him, he clutched the arm tightly. When Wilson saw me walking across the parking lot, he started to verbally harass me.

"Hey, you the same woman at the house with that gun? You don't look the same, baby. You lookin' real good to me now. I love tough women. You know you like me. Hey, you think you too good for me? I'll show you who's too good . . ."

He grabbed Detrin and knocked him down like a madman. He jumped on top of him, pinned him to the ground, and held his hands to his throat.

I took the baton and tried to wedge it between Wilson and Detrin so I could pull Wilson off, but I couldn't get it in the right position. I whacked him on his back, head, and arms, but he acted as though he didn't feel it. I went to the front of him and tried to push him backwards, but that didn't work either. Wilson kept his death grip on Detrin's throat. Time was running out. Detrin's face turned purplish-blue, and I thought he might pass out.

Fearing for Detrin's life, I pulled my revolver. But I couldn't pull the trigger. If I shot Wilson in the back, chances were great the bullet would go right through him and into Detrin. I pressed the muzzle of my gun against the back of Wilson's head and said, "Let him go or I'm going to pull this trigger."

Wilson whipped his left arm around with such force that he knocked the gun out of my hand and across the parking lot. Before I could pull away, Wilson grabbed my right arm and twisted it like it was putty. I punched and kicked him, but he remained unfazed.

"Let go! Stop!" I cried through clenched teeth.

"Try to shoot me now," he taunted.

Then he bit my thumb so hard I thought he had severed it. The intense pain made me feel as if I were going into shock. *Father God, please help me,* I prayed.

Momentarily, I wondered if Detrin was still alive. The pain numbed my mind.

Then I heard the sirens and the police cars careening into the parking lot. Officers ran to our assistance, pulled Wilson away, and freed my arm.

I sank to the pavement and watched as ten officers attended to Detrin and handcuffed Wilson.

An officer picked me up and placed me in an ambulance. Later I would discover that all the tendons in my right arm from my wrist to my elbow had been torn, and my thumb was dislocated.

I don't remember the ambulance ride or being carried into the hospital emergency room. As a matter of fact, I don't remember anything about the hospital stay.

I have no idea how much time had passed before I opened my eyes again, but I could hardly believe what I saw. I was in my old bedroom in my father's house. The greatest comfort was to see my father sitting beside my bed, watching over me. His weary eyes told me he'd been there all night. He wanted to be the first to greet me and to welcome me home.

Just as I opened my eyes to my earthly father, someday I will fall asleep and awaken to another familiar place. Familiar because of the presence of loved ones who have gone before me, and also because I will be in my heavenly Father's house. I know I will recognize my Father, sitting beside me, watching over me, waiting to welcome me home.

SECTION *Ten*

The EMBRACE OF A FATHER

MY FIRST BROKEN HEART

STEPHEN R. COVEY

from *Living the Seven Habits*

Just as air is the deepest hunger of the human body, to be understood (Habit 5: Seek First to Understand, Then to Be Understood) is the deepest hunger of the human heart. Notice in this story the power of unconditional love, how simply understanding can heal.

When I was seventeen years old, I suffered my first romantic heartbreak. I will never forget the pain of that experience. The girl I had been dating, without warning and without mercy, broke off our relationship and immediately began dating a close friend. In one moment, my world came crashing down. I remember driving my 1952 Willys jeep out into the hills above my hometown of Redlands, California, determined that I would never, ever go back to school, or life, again. Finally, as evening set, hunger and pain drove me home. I said little, but the look in my eyes must have told my parents what happened. I could not eat, so I went into my bedroom, fell into bed, and began to weep. I sobbed and sobbed. After some time, the door of my bedroom quietly opened, and I sensed the presence of my father standing quietly by my bed. Gently, he pulled back the covers of my bed and climbed in beside me. He wrapped me in his strong, warm arms and held me closer than I have ever been held in my life. He pulled my heart, my body, my spirit into him. I felt his warmth and strength, as I continued to sob. And then, my father began to weep with me. I felt his chest shudder with his own sobs. His face was pressed into the side of mine, and I felt his warm tears leave his eyes and mingle with mine as they ran down my cheek. He said nothing. He just wept. Wept because I was in pain. Wept because he loved me and felt my pain. After long moments, my sobs began to subside and a growing light replaced the pain. My father got up, tucked the blankets around my chin, and rested his hand on my shoulder. He then said, "My son, I promise the sun will come out again. I love you." He then left as quietly as he entered. He was right. The sun did come out. I arose, dressed my best, polished my jeep, and headed for school.

Life went on, richer than before somehow, for I knew I was loved, unconditionally, by a father who taught me what empathy really means. Recently I quietly closed the lid on my father's casket. Before I did so, I paused, once more, to stroke the whiskers of his chin and remember that night, long ago.

––––––––––

Editor's Note: *Such profound emotional experiences last a lifetime and give powerful scripts to the next generation. My guess is that this person does the same thing with his children as his father did with him.*

STUCK IN A TIGHT PLACE

CLARK COTHERN

from Detours

Dad! *DAD!*"

Good grief, now what?

I was halfway up the stairs to my little office, intending to grab some much-needed study time. Before I could reach the top, however, Katheryn, my oldest daughter, came bounding up the stairs behind me, breathlessly delivering her usual tidings of great astonishment.

"Dad!" she yelled. "There's something in our fireplace!"

In the fireplace? Nah. Couldn't be. Probably just the wind rattling that loose slate below the door.

"Come *quick*, Daddy!" My youngest daughter, Callie, had joined in the race up the stairs and was quickly gaining on us.

I sighed, stopped on the top step—only a few feet away from precious solitude—and waited for my exuberant messengers to thunder up the stairs behind me. Looking down the hall, I could actually see my computer. I was *that* close.

All I'd wanted to do was escape to my desk in the corner of the upstairs bedroom and finish the week's Advent sermons. Here was yet another distraction, heaped like coal in my stocking in this already too-busy time of year.

With a sigh, I figured the only way to get rid of this distraction was to prove there was nothing in the fireplace. Ridiculous. This was nothing more than premature visions of dancing sugarplums—or however the poem went. It was obvious the kids were not going to let me go to work until I had investigated their claims. I resigned myself to the two-minute trip all the way back down two flights of stairs to the basement, where I would open the doors and show them the empty fireplace. Case closed.

Then I could put the latest crisis to rest and get on with the business of helping people learn how to slow down, get rid of their stress, and appreciate the real meaning of the season. *Ha.* I laughed at the irony. *Physician, heal thyself!*

Somewhere between floors, our little parade picked up my son, so I arrived in the basement with three kids clinging to my pants legs like static-charged socks out of the dryer. It's amazing how they can get each other pumped up. All it takes is one false alarm and . . .

Good gracious, they were right. There really IS something in our fireplace. Something alive and kicking.

I saw its eye peering at me through the crack in the door panel. At my approach, I could hear the sound of claws scratching at the door.

"Well, I'll be," I said, shaking my head in disbelief.

The kids were jumping up and down, yelling, "Told you! Told you!"

Yeah, yeah. They'd told me. It's tough to be wrong when you're the parent. There couldn't be anything in our fireplace, but there was. Quickly moving past denial and into acceptance, I said, "Whatever it is, it must have had a wild ride down that chimney—what with those bends and the drop onto the smoke shelf."

"What IS it?" the kids demanded.

This unexpected turn of events was becoming curiouser and curiouser. I had heard of bats flying into chimneys—or an occasional owl. Maybe this was Dr. Seuss's grinch, out to steal our Christmas. Trying to get eyeball to eyeball with the critter, I leaned a bit closer.

"I dunno," I admitted. "I can't quite tell *what* it is."

It was too small to be a raccoon, but too large to be a bird. And that beady animal eye! It was kind of eerie. I gingerly reached my finger toward the crack in the opening to see how friendly it might be.

"D-a-a-d," Clarkie said in a shaky voice, "Dad, I don't think you should do that."

"It's okay," I told him. "I'm just going to see if it might be—you know, tame. Maybe it's somebody's cat that got up on the roof." I could feel little Callie trembling as she clung to my leg, hiding her body behind mine, only peeking out enough to see what was going on.

This was serious stuff, Dad going one on one with a mysterious invader. Truth be told, I felt a little queasy about getting too close. But hey, I'm the dad. Dads aren't afraid of anything, right? I had to make a good show of courage for the sake of the children.

Just as I began to draw near, however, the creature went nuts—darting around, bumping into the doors, making a ghastly racket. I yanked my hand back as if I'd just stuck my finger into a light socket.

Clarkie started to say something, but I cut him off at the pass. "I know, I know, you told me. I shouldn't have done that."

Just then I caught sight of the animal's brown and bushy tail . . . and that gave it away. When it came back around to the door and stuck its nose in the crack, I could tell what kind of animal we were dealing with.

"It's a squirrel," I announced, grateful to be right about at least one thing.

"Whoa." All three kids spoke in unison, as though on cue.

Katheryn: "Good thing we didn't have a fire going, huh, Dad?"

Clarkie: "Can we keep it?"

Callie: "Yeah, Dad, can we . . . *please?*"

Dad: "Let me think about it. Okay, I've thought about it. NO!"

Like other unexpected holiday guests we've encountered throughout the years, this one required a bit of extra attention. Ah, those detours. They can certainly arrive in the most unexpected packages.

I spoke to it softly, trying to calm it down. "Sorry, friend, no room within. Anyway, you wouldn't like this place. Gets kinda warm sometimes. I'm afraid you'll have to spend the night out behind the garage, or up a tree . . . or wherever it is adventurous squirrels sack out.

"Look how cute it is, kids. Maybe, if it knows we're not going to hurt it, I could just reach in and gently lift it out." I thought it might calm down after its first blast of frenetic energy. But no sooner had the last word left my mouth than it began scratching about like a squirrel overdosed on espresso.

I yanked my hand back again.

"Or not," I added quickly.

I recalled a story my neighbor had told about these seemingly innocent little squirrels ripping houses apart. So what might it do to an overly forward preacher?

The kids and I considered our options:

(1) We could anesthetize it with the vapors of the starter fluid we had for the old van. That stuff was basically just ether in a spray can. *Nope,* I reasoned. *With our luck we'd all go clunk on the floor with the varmint scurrying over our unconscious bodies and stealing all the nuts out of the candy dish.*

(2) We could tie a garbage bag around the door area to the wood burner, open up the doors and let the squirrel run into the bag. Nix that one. It might suffocate. And besides, those plastic bags aren't very thick. Kinda wimpy. We'd end up with a wild-eyed squirrel residing in the basement rather than the fireplace. On to plan three.

(3) We could cut a squirrel-sized hole in the side of a cardboard box, place the box next to the door, and gently slide up the slate on the door, creating a nifty little squirrel corridor into the box. It would be just like walking from the gantry elevator into the space shuttle.

Eureka! No vote had to be taken. When I mentioned that idea, eyebrows went up and heads nodded all around. We were of one mind, then. We just *knew* it was the right thing to do.

Clarkie took off to find a box in the attic. Katheryn ran upstairs to barricade the kitchen (in case Plan Three bombed), and Callie shook with nervousness at the top of the stairs. (Oh, she of little faith. Alas, every team has its skeptic.) Joy decided her battle station was near Callie, who needed some consolation that Daddy was not going to make some dumb mistake and send the squirrel scampering about the living room. (I wasn't sure who had less faith in this operation, Callie or her mother.)

So, with Ma in her kerchief and I in my cap, I got out the pliers and set the squirrel trap.

It took some doing, but I jiggled loose the slate from its place in the door, all the while keeping an eye on the skittish little bolt of lightning on the other side. When I got the box in place, I slid up the slate s-l-o-w-l-y—until . . . ahhh . . . ever so gently, the squirrel waltzed right into the box, just as though we'd been practicing this docking maneuver for weeks.

Sliding a piece of cardboard down to cover the hole, I took hold of the box, keeping an eye out for little squirrel appendages that might find their way out of cracks in the top. It seemed content to be still, though, and I was grateful. Because if it had started ripping around in that box, I'm not sure I would have made it to the top of the stairs without dropping it out of sheer terror.

The kids watched breathlessly, keeping their fingers crossed as I approached the side door to the house, which my son had held open, stepping well out of the way so as not to trip his old dad.

We all let out a collective sigh of relief when I stepped over the threshold and out into the open air. I walked to the backyard, set the box down on the grass, and removed the cardboard, exposing the entrance-turned-exit. We all stood across the yard, watching, waiting, wondering why the squirrel was taking so long to leave when the way seemed so clear.

After about a minute, our guest stuck its little nose out, sniffing, making that nervous little squirrel face that makes them seem so innocent and cute. It paused a moment, took about three tentative steps just outside the box, stopped, turned around to look at us as if to say, "Thanks, blokes. Top o' the mornin' to ya," and then scampered away, a bit sootier and a tad wiser for the experience.

I accepted the applause of my three appreciative children and then headed back upstairs, hoping for at least a few moments of quiet before the next detour called me away from my Advent meditations.

Finally, I found the solitude I'd been seeking. Not a creature was stirring, not even a . . . squirrel.

Wouldn't you just know it, all I could think about was that crazy squirrel. In spite of myself, I couldn't help but reflect on this most recent detour from my sermon preparations. *Isn't it funny,* I thought, *how, before we had rushed to its redemption, our little visitor had frantically tried to bash its way out of its dark prison inside the wood burner?* It seemed that the harder it struggled to get free, the more pain it caused itself. It was sooty black, frightened, exhausted.

In the end, he simply had to wait patiently until one who was much bigger—one who could peer into his world—could carry him safely to that larger world where he really belonged. *Hmm,* I thought, *maybe there's a purpose in this detour after all.*

I began writing the experience we had just witnessed as an illustration for the following Sunday's sermon.

"When the first Christmas took place," I mused, "many people on earth had fallen into the dark prison of sin. The harder they tried to bash their way out of their confines, the more they hurt themselves. In fact, they could not escape. Unless a more powerful someone came from the outside, they were trapped and in despair.

"As the carol says, 'Long lay the world, in sin and error pining, till *He* appeared . . . and the soul felt its worth.' "

What did the Scriptures say?

> For he has rescued us from the dominion of darkness and brought us into the kingdom of the Son he loves, in whom we have redemption, the forgiveness of sins. (Colossians 1:13–14)

Yeah, this'll preach, I told myself.

"All they had to do was simply relax and allow the person who was so much bigger than they were to carry them to safety in a world where they really belonged."

SEWN AND STUFFED, INC.

RUSTY FISCHER

My dad called them dolls, but they weren't. Not really. I called them "stuffed people," because, even though I was only eight, I knew boys weren't supposed to play with dolls.

My grandmother had taught me how to sew when I was only seven, and sometimes it was easier to make my own teddy bear or superhero out of felt and a pair of those funny googly eyes than to save up my allowance and walk all the way to our local Toy King for the real thing.

After a while I had all kinds of stuffed people, although few of them were actually people. There were horses for the cowboys. Bears to keep Grizzly Adams company. Big red dragons to fight the gray felt knights. My mom admired each new creation that I made so much that she finally started putting them on a shelf where I couldn't reach them.

"They're too nice to play with," she'd say, handing me new sheets of colored felt and thread she'd picked up at the craft store. "Now, let's see what you can make out of these."

By the time Thanksgiving rolled around, the knights and horses, cowboys and dragons had so crowded the shelves that there was no room for any more! Mom knew something had to be done when a stuffed ghost left over from Halloween fell from the shelf and got stuck in her hair.

"I know," she said, the same gleam in her eye she had when she suggested I start my own lemonade stand, and all I got for my trouble was a sunburn and twenty-three fire ant bites. "Why don't you make a cardboard display, and we'll take them down to the restaurant? Your dad can sell them by the cash register."

That suggestion sounded like a great idea. So I found a large box and went to work with my watercolors to make the display. By the end of that morning, even though I hadn't realized it, Sewn and Stuffed, Inc. was born.

Mom and I drove to my dad's restaurant and showed him my display. Although I knew he wasn't the biggest fan of my dolls, he agreed to put them by the cash register. He moved the big rack of salted nuts and breath mints and put my horses, dragons, ghosts, and reindeer there instead.

I'd never been so proud. Then the money started rolling in, and I realized what proud *really* meant.

Dad charged three dollars for each stuffed person and four for each stuffed animal or monster. By the end of the first day he brought a twenty-dollar bill home and handed it to me with a flourish. I ran out right away and bought more felt, thread, and real stuffing to replace the newspaper and dishrags I had been using.

I sewed all night, trying to keep up with my first taste of supply and demand. Dad brought my new creations into work with him the next morning and came home eight hours later with another twenty-dollar bill.

The next day, on my way home from the craft store with a backpack full of more thread and felt, I took a detour to the restaurant to tell my dad how much I appreciated what he'd done for me.

I walked in and saw him pouring drinks for his customers, laughing and enjoying their banter. He waved at me, introduced me all around, and asked why the unexpected visit. I certainly couldn't tell him with all those strangers around, so I just smiled and told him I wanted to say hi, that's all.

Then I slipped into his business office to write him a note on his thick, blue stationery. It was then that I realized my dad must be too embarrassed to actually sell my stuffed creations. What I saw made me realize that it was possible for a parent to lie to a child. All of Sewn and Stuffed, Inc.'s animals, men, knights, and monsters were piled on one of the chairs across from his desk, spilling out of the cardboard and water-color sales rack that was supposed to be next to the cash register. It was obvious, even to a fool as big as I obviously was, that Dad was just tossing my dolls over here, and bringing me home one of his own twenty-dollar bills each night!

I don't know how I made it home that day with the tears pouring down my face and blurring my eyes. I cried myself to sleep long before Dad ever got home. The next morning, however, there he was, sitting on the edge of my bed.

I rubbed my eyes and saw that he was already dressed in his shirt and tie, ready for another big day at his restaurant. I should have been getting up too, but I knew Sewn and Stuffed, Inc. wouldn't be needing fresh supplies anytime soon.

"Listen, son," he said quietly. "Your mother told me all about what happened yesterday. But it's not what you think. I did sell some of your doll . . . er . . . your stuffed creations. And the customers raved about them. They really did. But after a while, I didn't want to let any more of them go.

"You put so much time and effort into them," he continued, stroking my head in the early morning light. "I just knew those strangers wouldn't appreciate them as much as I did. So I bought the rest of them. They're in my office, where they'll stay. I'm going to get one of my handy employees to build me a proper shelf."

He didn't have to wait long. Underneath the Christmas tree that year was a set of shelves I had made myself. They weren't all that straight, and I ran out of sandpaper on Christmas Eve before they were entirely smooth, but they went up in his office the very next day. Dad never complained about them once. And they remain there to this day. They're a little dusty, somewhat faded, and slightly crooked. But they're more than strong enough to hold Sewn and Stuffed, Inc.'s first quarter production inventory.

Needless to say, my business soon went belly up. Needles and thread and felt gave way to soccer balls and catcher's mitts. But I often reflect upon my very first business venture. And I still consider it a glowing success, despite what the well-balanced spreadsheet might say:

Cost of materials: $40.

Earnings: $40.

Gross profit on return: priceless.

THE FIFTEEN-CENT-GLIDER DAD

DOUGLAS KNOX

When we were younger, my brother, Mark, and I understood that our family didn't have a lot of money, but we were spared the details of how desperate things were for Dad and Mom. Dad left for work at Archway Bakery before we got up in the morning, and didn't come home until long after our school day ended. They also spared us the details of the difficulties Mom had bringing our little sister, Beth, into the world, of their subsistence-level income, and of Dad's refusal to take a much higher paying position at a rival bakery because he would not compromise his principles by sharing the cookie recipes he had memorized.

In his absence, Dad made his presence known by a roof over our heads, food on the table, and two pairs of new shoes every school year—tennis shoes for gym, and good shoes to be shared between school and church. He never let us go hungry, even when it meant taking on occasional part-time jobs on top of his regular work.

Having taken those things for granted, I asked simpler questions. When I struggled with a relatively short day at school, I used to wonder how he had so much stamina. I didn't understand that it was his intense sense of responsibility for his family that drove him to work those Herculean hours to keep us alive and spare Mom the necessity of having to work outside the house. We learned instead to expect a lot of love, not to count on too many material possessions, and to appreciate the little things.

The occasional Saturdays when Dad was home were a real treat. But none matched that magical Saturday when he came back from the store with three small, elongated plastic bags, stapled at the top with a single folded piece of cardboard that had a picture on the front and assembly instructions on the back.

It was the weekend of the fifteen-cent-balsa-wood gliders.

They were U.S. Air Force gliders, complete with guns printed on the fuselage and red and blue chevrons stamped on the wings. Mark and I knew we could shoot down anything in the sky with them. The most special thing was that Dad had gotten them for us.

We asked a hundred questions: "Can we put them together now? Can gliders made of wood really fly? How do you know where the parts go? What's the metal thing on the front? Why is the slot for the wings wider than the wings? Can we take them out right away?"

Dad coached us on how fragile they were—they were not toys that we could smash around—and patiently answered all our questions while he showed us how to assemble them. Then he took us to a field up the street from where we lived.

I don't know how long we were there, but we learned everything there was to know about flying balsa gliders that day.

"Put your pointer finger on the back of the plane when you hold it," Dad told us, "and it will fly better."

Boy, did they ever.

They flew almost twice as far with the extra leverage. We laughed and ran through the field, chasing after our jet fighters. Then Dad introduced us to the finer points of aerodynamics. The wide slot for the wings was something they did on purpose. Pushing the wings forward made them go on long flights, but if we pulled them back they would do loop-de-loops. He positioned the wings on his glider and let fly, and his plane flew a loop that couldn't have been more than fifteen feet at the apex. It rushed past him on the bottom of the dive, started a second loop, stalled when it lost momentum, and regained just enough lift to level out just a few feet in front of him and land belly down on the ground.

Mark and I knew we were invincible. We experimented with every conceivable position of the wings until we were sure we could conquer any imaginary enemy or land on any terrain.

Then Dad showed us the greatest maneuver of all. He pulled the wings on his plane back to the rearward position, and gave a sidearm heave. The plane turned an almost complete circle on a near-ninety degree bank, not more than four feet above the ground. We were awestruck. I don't know if Dad knew the plane was going to do that or if it was a spur-of-the-moment idea, but it was the Top Gun flight of the day.

That day Dad had spent forty-five cents on three dime-store relics and turned the day into something priceless.

The sheer simplicity of that Saturday has never left me. After I grew up and raised my own family, I found that life can become far more complicated than any kid could imagine. I've sweated over the next house payment, worried more about how we would afford emergency medical bills than the emergencies themselves, tried to be a provider on a job that paid little more than minimum wage, and agonized at times whether we were doing enough for our girls. I wonder if Dad felt the same frustration I did, if he felt those cheap balsa gliders were a poor expression of the love he had for us. Whether he did or not, to Mark and me it was an afternoon of pure delight.

A HIGHER PLACE

WAYNE HOLMES

E ach summer my mom and dad loaded the family car, and we made the long, are-we-there-yet and how-much-longer trip to the mountains and hills of southwest Virginia and Mamaw's house.

For the most part, these trips bored my two brothers and me. We spent the long hours riding in the car bickering with one another, while our parents barked orders to knock it off.

Over time a few memories have helped me to see the importance of family. Hunting in the woods, fishing in the creek, playing hide-and-seek in the barn, and other cherished memories have allowed me to appreciate the heritage my parents gave me.

One memory stands out.

As far as I know, the mountain had no name. It was just one among many, but it was special to me because it was the mass I saw while standing on my grandmother's front porch. It loomed over us like a mighty fortress—a stronghold—a citadel high on a hill. Its tree-lined top made the sheer rock front look like a blank face with hair on top. The precipice intrigued me. It beckoned me to come and conquer its heights.

At the age of twelve, I was too young to meet the challenge on my own. But it wasn't beyond the capabilities of my father. He could climb its steep trails, traverse its peaks, and overcome the perils of wildlife.

I was elated the day my dad asked if my brother and I would like to join him and my uncle on a journey to the top of the mountain.

"It'll be a lot of work, and we'll have to spend the night in a little cabin at the top," my father explained. "It's too long a trip to go up and down all in one day."

Would I like to go? Absolutely, positively—YES! What an adventure this will be, I thought.

The next morning, after my mom and grandmother had seen to it that we'd been properly fed, we piled into the car and headed for the base of the mountain. My excitement was high, but not wanting to come across as childish—and ruin my chances of tagging along—I tried to contain my elation.

My young mind had failed to realize the difficulty of the journey. The mountain was too steep to approach head-on. Instead, we would climb a nearby mountain that was not as steep and then travel across the tableland to reach our destination.

With confident spirits, joyous hearts, and a song on our lips, we began. I don't know what I was expecting, but the journey wasn't what I thought it would be. The constant climbing, up and up and up, was far from fun. Even though Dad had said it would be a lot of work, it never really dawned on me that climbing a mountain could be that hard. It was the hardest work I'd ever undertaken.

My father, however, appeared unfazed. He climbed steadily, chatting with my uncle as if it were a casual Sunday stroll.

"Stay close, boys," he said to us, "never know when you might stumble on a wild animal or a snake."

Snake? Were there snakes in the neighborhood? I wondered.

"Poisonous snakes?" I asked.

"Yeah, they've seen a few around. But if you don't bother them, they won't bother you. You just don't want to stumble on one accidentally and startle it. No tellin' what it might do."

Great! I thought. *Now I have to watch every step I take.*

At that point I fell in behind my father. I figured he could lead the way and clear the path for us. If snakes were around, he could deal with them.

After what seemed like days of uphill climbing we finally reached a summit. My dad decided it was time to take a break. I'd made that decision long before he did, but I didn't want to come across as a whiner.

"Let's catch our breath. We're going to need it for the rest of the journey," he said.

I couldn't believe what I was hearing. It sounded like my dad was saying the worst was yet to come. I was tired, sore, and wanted to go home. Instead, I got a ten-minute respite before beginning our journey again.

The next part of the trip wasn't uphill. We had crested the first mountain and moved across the top of the mountain ridge. Though the second half of the climb wasn't as physically challenging, the distance made the trip long and hard, especially since the first half had taken so much energy.

We did come across one snake on our hike, and yes, it was poisonous. But, true to my father's words, we didn't bother it, and it didn't bother us. Apparently we each had our own path to take.

As evening drew near, we finally reached our destination. High on top of the world stood a rustic old cabin. No electricity, no running water, and no indoor bathroom, but it was the most welcome sight I'd seen on the journey—a shelter from the elements and protection from wildlife.

Not far from the cabin was the most spectacular view I'd ever seen. It seemed the entire world lay at my feet, sprawled out before me like miniature houses and farms on a child's board game. I spotted my grandmother's house and tiny cars parked in the yard. I saw fields squarely dotting the countryside and roads winding serpent-like through the hills and valleys. Nature's beauty was spread before me, and, even at the young age of twelve, I was enchanted by its grandeur.

———

Over the years, reflecting on that day has given me some insights on life. I learned that life is not just a destination but a journey. While the expedition can be long and arduous, it can be full of beauty and pleasure as well.

My dad's leadership role that day reminds me that my heavenly Father also invites me on an adventure to a higher place. And, like my dad, he leads me, watches over me, protects me, calls me to rest, and assures me we will arrive together.

Yes, the pilgrimage can be long and hard. Some days the trek is much more difficult than I ever imagined. But just as I was thrilled to be climbing together with my dad, so I am thrilled to know that God walks beside me day by day.

I've also discovered that the higher I go, the better the view. The problems of life seem Lilliputian when viewed from the mountaintop.

AND GRACE MY FEARS RELIEVED

WALTER WANGERIN, JR.

from *Little Lamb, Who Made Thee?*

First of all the love of God is a terrible thing. It begins by revealing unto us such treacheries and threats in the world that we know we must die soon—and until then (we are sure) we shall live in continual terror of the end to come.

The first act of divine love is to persuade us of the reality of death. We shudder and doubt that this can be love. We hate the messenger. We loathe such lovers. But it is a dear, necessary act nonetheless, because without it the second act of God's love would be altogether meaningless to us.

The second act is mercy. An absurdity of mercy. It is that God himself enters the same reality he first revealed unto us; he bows down and joins us under the same threat of death—and those whom he taught to fear he leads to safety. But those who do not fear do not follow. See? We had to suffer extremest fright in order to know our extreme need.

We who are under death must admit the peril; we have no other choice—except to die. Except to die.

But God, who exists above death, who knows no need at all, had the choice that we did not have. If, then, he emptied himself of power and humbled himself to death—even to death on a cross—this was purely an act of mercy on our behalf.

Then who can measure the love of God, to be thrice sacrificed: first, to be despised for declaring the terrible truth; second, to descend by choice into this treacherous and transient world; third, to save us by dying indeed the death he had revealed, dying it in our stead? Or whereto shall we liken so violent, valiant, and near an approach of the kingdom of heaven unto us?

Well—

The coming of the kingdom is like the coming of my father to my brothers and me when we sat fishing, blithely fishing, from a ledge twelve feet above the water in a stony cove in Glacier National Park.

In that year of sudden awakening, 1954, I was ten. My brothers, grinning idiots all (for that they followed a fool) were, in descending order, nine and seven and six.

Just before our trip west, I had furnished myself with fishing equipment. A Cheerios box top and my personal dime had purchased ten small hooks, three flies, leader, line, a red-and-white bobber, and three thin pieces of bamboo, which fit snugly into one pole. Such a deal! Such a shrewd fellow I felt myself to be.

A leader of brothers indeed.

On a bright blue morning we chopped bits of bacon into a pouch, left the tent on high ground, and went forth fishing and to fish. We sought a mountain stream, though we ourselves did not depart the trail down from the campground. Fortunately, that same trail became a wooden bridge, which crossed furious roaring waters, the crashing of a falls from the slower bed of a stream.

A mountain stream! There, to our right, before it dived down into the rocky chasm below this bridge, was a mountain stream. Filled with fishes, certainly. We had found it.

But the bridge joined two high walls of stone, and even the slower stream came through a narrow defile.

But I was a shrewd fellow in those days, a leader, like I said. I noticed that a narrow ledge snaked away from the far end of the bridge, that it went beneath the belly of a huge boulder and therefore was hidden from the view of lesser scouts. If we could crawl that ledge on hands and knees through its narrowest part, ducking low for the boulder, why, we'd come to a widening, a hemisphere of stone big enough to sit on, from which to dangle our legs, a sort of fortress of stone since the wall went up from that ledge a flat twelve feet and down again from that ledge another twelve feet. Perfect. Safe from attacks. Good for fishing.

I led my blinking brothers thither. None questioned me. I was the oldest. Besides, I was the one with foresight enough to have purchased a fishing pole.

"You got to flatten out here," I called back, grunting in order to fit beneath the outcropping boulder. They did. One by one they arrived with me in a fine, round hideout. Above the sheer rock some trees leaned over and looked down upon us. Below our feet there turned a lucid pool of water, itself some twelve feet deep.

And so the Brothers Wangerin, Sons of Gladness and Glory, began to spend a fine day fishing.

We took turns with the pole.

The bacon didn't work, but—as a sign of our favor with all the world—the trees dropped down on silken threads some tiny green worms, exactly the size of our tiny hooks. We reached out and plucked worms from the air, baited the hooks, and caught (truly, truly) several fingerling fish. Oh, it was a good day! All that we needed we had.

Then came my father.

We didn't see him at first. We weren't thinking about him, so filled with ourselves were we, our chatting and our various successes.

But I heard through the water's roar a cry.

Distant, distant: *Wally!*

I glanced up and to my right—where the water dropped over stone, where the bridge arched it—and I almost glanced away again, but a wild waving caught my eye.

WALLY! WALLY! WALLY!

"Dad?" Yes!—it was Dad. "Hey, look, you guys. There's Dad leaning over the bridge."

They all looked, and straightway Philip started to cry, and then Mike, too. Paul dropped my pole into the water twelve feet below. And I saw in our father's eyes a terror I had never seen before.

WALLY, HOW DID YOU GET OVER THERE?

Over here? I looked around.

Suddenly *here* was no fortress at all. It was a precipice, a sheer stone drop to a drowning water, and *that* water rushed toward a thundering falls far, far below my father. With his eyes I saw what I had not seen before. In his seeing (which loved us terribly) I saw our peril.

He was crying out as loud as he could: *WALLY, COME HERE! COME HERE!*

But the ledge by which we'd come had shrunk. It was thin as a lip now. The hairs on my neck had started to tingle, and my butt grew roots. I couldn't move. Neither did my brothers. I didn't even shake my head. I was afraid that any motion at all would pitch me headlong into the pool below. I gaped at my father, speechless.

He stopped waving. He lowered his arms and stopped shouting. He stood for an eternal moment looking at us from the bridge, and then his mouth formed the word, *Wait.* We couldn't hear it. He didn't lift his voice. Quietly under the booming waters he whispered, *Wait.*

Then he bent down and removed his shoes. At the near end of the bridge, he bent down farther, farther, until he was on his stomach, worming forward, knocking dust and pebbles by his body into the stream, bowing beneath the enormous boulder that blocked our freedom.

"Dad's coming. See him?"

"Yep, Dad's coming."

"I knew he would."

He pulled himself ahead on the points of his elbows, like the infantry beneath barbed wire, his face drawn and anxious. He was wearing shorts and a long-sleeved flannel shirt. Red with darker red squares. I remember.

When he came into our tiny cove, he turned on his belly and hissed to the youngest of us, "Mike, take my heel." Mike was six. He didn't.

"Mike, *now!*" Dad shouted above the waterfall with real anger. "Grab my heel in your hand and follow me."

You should know that my father is by nature and breeding a formal man. I don't recall that he often appeared in public wearing short-sleeved shirts. Nor would he permit people to call him by his first name, asking rather that they address him according to his position, his title and degree. Even today the most familiar name he will respond to is "Doc." Dad is two-legged and upright. Dad is organized, controlled, clean, precise, dignified, decorous, civil—and formal.

What a descent it was, therefore, and what a sweet humiliation, that he should on his stomach scrabble this way and that, coming on stone then going again, pulling after him one son after the other: Michael, Philip, Paul.

And then me.

"Wally, grab my heel. Follow me."

It wasn't he who had put us in these straits. Nevertheless, he chose to enter them with us, in order to take us out with him. It was foolishness that put us here. It was love that brought him.

So he measured the motion of his long leg by the length of my small arm, and he never pulled farther than I could reach. The waters roared and were troubled; the granite shook with the swelling thereof. But my father was present, and very present. I felt the flesh of his heel in my hand, leading me; and I was still in my soul. I ceased to be afraid.

That stony cove had not been a refuge at all but a danger. Rather, my father in love bore refuge unto me; my father bore me back to safety again. So I did not die in the day of my great stupidity. I lived.

Thus is the kingdom of heaven likened unto a certain man whose eldest son was a nincompoop—

PERMISSIONS AND ACKNOWLEDGMENTS

Every effort has been made to secure proper permission and acknowledgment for each story in this work. If an error has been made, please accept my apologies and contact Bethany House Publishers, 11400 Hampshire Ave. So., Bloomington, MN 55438, so that corrections can be made in future editions.

Permission to reprint any of the stories from this book must be obtained from the original source. Acknowledgments are listed by story title in the order they appear in the book. Heartfelt thanks to all the authors and publishers who allowed their work to be included in this collection.

The Unconditional Love of a Father

"The Reunion," *In the Grip of Grace* by Max Lucado. Copyright © 1996, Word Publishing, Nashville, Tennessee. All rights reserved.

"Truant Tears" by C. Vernon Hostetler. Copyright © 2001. Used by permission. All rights reserved. C. Vernon Hostetler has been a pastor, an alcoholic rehabilitation counselor, a salesman, and an entrepreneur. His three sons are all engaged in Christian ministry. He has been twice widowed, and currently lives in Cincinnati, Ohio.

"Longer, Daddy, Longer . . ." excerpted from *Leaving the Light On* © 1994 by Gary Smalley and John Trent, Ph.D. Used by permission of Multnomah Publishers, Inc.

"I Was on His Mind" by Michael J. Massie. Copyright © 2001. Used by permission. All rights reserved. Michael Massie has a bachelor's degree in English education from Miami University and a master of divinity in theological studies from Anderson University School of Theology. Michael is pursuing a career as a professor of biblical studies. He and his wife, Kelly, live in Anderson, Indiana.

"Father-in-Law Love" by Linda E. Knight. Copyright © 2001. Used by permission. All rights reserved. Linda E. Knight is a writer and poet and is currently writing the *Chucky and Gordy* stories and songs for Faithville Gospelcast Production/Kid's TV. She is the mother of three grown sons and lives in Woodslee, Ontario, Canada, with her husband.

"See You at the House," excerpted from *See You at the House*, selected and edited

The Wisdom of a Father

The Discipline of a Father

The Teaching of a Father

and a writer by night. She still uses her father's tools but has since purchased a toolbox.

The Forgiveness of a Father

"A Home, a Gift," excerpted from *In the Heart of the World: Thoughts, Stories and Prayers* by Mother Teresa. Copyright © 1998. Reprinted with permission of New World Library, Novato, CA 94949, *www.nwlib.com.*

"The Father's Love" by Dan Thiessen. Copyright © 2001. Used by permission. All rights reserved. Dan Thiessen is a husband, father, and pastor of Hosanna Christian Fellowship in Ottawa, Ontario. Dan loves writing about the father-heart of God, helping people to understand God's character and nature. He is also a Christian recording artist with four original projects; the latest is entitled *I Stand.*

"At the Father's Table" by Bob Hostetler. Copyright © 2001. Used by permission. All rights reserved. Bob Hostetler is a writer, editor, pastor, and speaker from southwestern Ohio. His thirteen books include *They Call Me A.W.O.L.* and *Holy Moses (and Other Adventures in Vertical Living).* He and his wife, Robin, are among the leaders of Cobblestone Community Church in Oxford, Ohio. They have two children, Aubrey and Aaron, and live near Oxford, Ohio.

"Restoration" by Elizabeth Marvin. Copyright © 2001. Used by permission. All rights reserved. Elizabeth Marvin lives in Ohio with her husband and two teenage children. A former teacher, she spends much of her spare time writing now that her kids are nearly grown. She enjoys leading women's Bible studies, reading, traveling, and taking long walks with her dog.

"I'm Sorry!" taken from *The Be-Happy Attitudes* by Robert H. Schuller. Copyright © 1985, Word Publishing, Nashville, Tennessee. All rights reserved.

"Abba, Daddy" by Lilly Green. Copyright © 2001. Used by permission. All rights reserved. Lilly Green lives in California with her husband, Kelly, and four sons. She has been a professional recording artist and songwriter and is currently following a lifelong passion for writing. Thankful for her rich Christian heritage, Lilly has found joy in honoring her dad and mom in musical tributes and stories.

The Perspective of a Father

"Seeing What Eyes Can't," taken from *When God Whispers Your Name* by Max Lucado. Copyright © 1994, Word Publishing, Nashville, Tennessee. All rights reserved.

The Provision of a Father

The Comfort of a Father

"A Rooted Life," from *Living Faith* by Jimmy Carter. Copyright © 1996 by Jimmy Carter. Adapted and used by permission of Times Books, a division of Random House, Inc.

"Coming Alongside Our Kids," taken from *The Father Connection* by Josh McDowell. Broadman and Holman Publishers, Nashville, Tenn. Copyright © 1996 by Josh McDowell. All rights reserved. Used by permission.

"The Worst Game of My Life!" Reprinted with the permission of Simon & Schuster from *Living the Seven Habits* by Stephen R. Covey. Copyright © 1999 by Franklin Covey Co.

"A Time to Be Born," excerpted from *For Everything a Season* by Philip Gulley. Copyright © 1999 by Philip Gulley. Used by permission of Multnomah Publishers, Inc.

"The Sunset" by Elsa Kok Cinjée. Copyright © 2001. Used by permission. All rights reserved. Elsa Kok Cinjée is a freelance writer and speaker from Columbia, Missouri. She is a single parent and outdoor enthusiast. Her articles have appeared in Focus on the Family's *Single Parent Family Magazine, Woman's World,* and within the Chicken Soup series. She recently published a Bible study for hurting women.

"Fear No Evil . . . Except," taken from *In My Father's House* by Corrie ten Boom. Copyright © 1976 by Corrie ten Boom. Fleming H. Revell, a division of Baker Book House Company. Used by permission.

The Fellowship of a Father

"My Father's Hands" by Teresa Cleary. Copyright © 2001. Used by permission. All rights reserved. Teresa Cleary has published over 1300 articles in a wide variety of Christian magazines. Her work has also appeared in *WWJD? God Speaks* and *Stories for a Teen's Heart, Volumes 1 & 2.* Her first book, *Front Porch Reflections,* a women's devotional, was released in 1999.

"Presents and Presence," excerpted from *Front Porch Tales* © 1997 by Philip Gulley. Used by permission of Multnomah Publishers, Inc.

"The Rock of Gibraltar" by Gail E. B. Padilla. Copyright © 2000. Used by permission. All rights reserved. Gail E. B. Padilla, writer and award-winning

The Embrace of a Father